MANAGEMENT OF WORKING CAPITAL

STUDIES IN FINANCE AND ACCOUNTING

General Editors: M. J. Barron and D. W. Pearce

Published

Michael Firth: MANAGEMENT OF WORKING CAPITAL

Forthcoming

M. J. Barron: BUSINESS FINANCE THEORY
M. J. Barron: MATRIX MODELS FOR ACCOUNTING
Michael Firth: THE VALUATION OF SHARES AND THE EFFICIENT MARKETS THEORY
K. Midgley and R. G. Burns: INSTITUTIONS OF THE CAPITAL MARKET
Brian Quinn: MULTINATIONAL BUSINESS FINANCE AND ACCOUNTING
T. Ryan: PORTFOLIO ANALYSIS
R. W. Scapens: ACCOUNTING IN AN INFLATIONARY ENVIRONMENT
Charles Sutcliffe: ECONOMICS VERSUS ACCOUNTANCY

Management of Working Capital

MICHAEL FIRTH

Lecturer in the Department of Accountancy and Business Law, University of Stirling

M

First published 1976 by
THE MACMILLAN PRESS LTD
London and Basingstoke
Associated companies in New York Dublin
Melbourne Johannesburg and Madras

SBN 333 18709 1 (hard cover)
333 18710 5 (paper cover)

Typeset, printed and bound
in Great Britain by
REDWOOD BURN LIMITED
Trowbridge & Esher

Contents

General Editors' Preface

The last few years have been very exciting for research in finance and accounting. An enormous amount has happened, and in many cases traditional thinking and traditional solutions have been completely overthrown. At the same time it is quite clear that research into the theory and, perhaps even more important, into British empirical evidence will continue to accumulate rapidly. While this is fine for the researcher in his detailed specialist world, it is not so good for the student who wants to acquire a relatively straightforward but up-to-date overview of the subject.

The 'Macmillan Studies in Finance and Accounting' set out to provide short, reasonably critical surveys of the developments within the various specialist areas of business finance and accounting. The emphasis in each study is upon recent work, but each topic will generally be placed in a historical context so that the reader may see the logical development of thought through time. Selected bibliographies are provided to guide readers to more extensive works. Each study aims at a brief treatment of the salient problems in order to avoid clouding the issues in too much detailed argument.

Unfortunately it is inevitable that in a few areas the level of mathematics will be rather near the limit for some students. This is because the rigorous methods of statistics, econometrics and mathematical economics have made a considerable contribution to the research achievements in the subject. Thus, although all the authors in the series have tried hard to make their presentation as lucid as possible, there is a point beyond which mathematical arguments cannot be explained non-mathematically except at a superficial level. Nevertheless intuition can go a long way and many students, even with very little mathematical background, have found that the intrinsic fascination of the subject more than compensates for occasional difficulty.

M. J. Barron
D. W. Pearce

CHAPTER 1

Introduction to Working-Capital Management

The management and control of working capital is of vital importance to companies and forms a major workload function of the finance manager and accountant. By working capital, the commonly accepted descriptive term for these resources, we mean the company's investment in short-term assets; traditionally these relate to items coming under the balance-sheet heading of current assets (in practice, of course, all capital is working, whether invested in fixed or current assets). Thus inventories (stocks), accounts receivable (debtors), short-term investments and cash balances all come within the term working capital. (The words in brackets represent alternative descriptions of the asset; throughout this book these terms are used synonymously.) Apart from the efficient operation and control of these assets, the finance manager will also be concerned with their financing. In this the finance manager will be faced with numerous alternative sources, both short-term and long-term. Short-term financing is generally shown under the heading of current liabilities and includes items such as bank overdrafts and credit received from suppliers. The efficient financing of current assets by short-term liabilities also comes within the scope of working-capital management and is therefore included in the text.

In reading the book the following terms will be found useful:

working capital	– a general term
gross working capital	– total current assets
net working capital	– current assets minus current liabilities

This is the generally accepted terminology although some text books adopt different definitions. A frequently used description of working capital is 'circulating capital' or 'circulating assets'; this description follows from the short-term cash cycle of the firm which is described later. This terminology can be confusing, however, as in the long term all assets are involved in the cash cycle. Because of this, the description 'circulating assets' is not used.

Component Items

Net working capital consists of current assets minus current liabilities. Current assets are those which are used in the selling operation of the business and which are held for short periods of time. Sometimes they are defined as those that are expected to be converted into cash within one year and this, in fact, covers virtually all the items. Many firms have assets which they intend to keep for the long term although they are in an easily realisable form such as investments. Although these are not termed current assets they can be utilised in working-capital management as they can often be easily converted into cash (Chapter 4 covers cash and marketable securities). The major component items of current assets are set out below.

(*a*) *Inventories or stocks*. These are the materials, commodities or goods that the firm has at any moment in time and which are expected to be used in the firm's production process or be sold in the form of a finished product in the normal day-to-day operations of the business. Inventories include raw materials, bought-in components, finished goods, and products part-way through a manufacturing process (known as work in progress).

(*b*) *Debtors or accounts receivable*. These are short-term debts owed to the company. In the case of manufacturing and commercial firms debts receivable generally represent credit taken by their sales customers.

(*c*) *Prepayments or expenses paid in advance*. These represent expenses that have been paid for but for which the goods or service have not yet been received.

(*d*) *Short-term investments*. When a firm has short-term surplus cash, this is often invested in securities on which a rate of return is expected, either in the form of interest received or capital appreciation; these amounts may be certain (i.e. local-authority deposits) or uncertain (equity shares). If a company decides to invest for the long term then the investment will not be shown in current assets and its management will be kept separate. However, if the investment can be easily and quickly sold, for example Stock Exchange Securities, then the item can be included in some working-capital analyses.

(*e*) *Cash and bank balances*. Any large items of cash are generally held in the bank in either current accounts or deposit accounts. In some industries, such as retailing, large balances of physical cash may be kept. An additional item which is sometimes differentiated in accounts is cash-in-transit. This represents payments by debtors which have not yet been received by the firm; any long delays in the transit of cash can result in large amounts of interest being forgone.

Current liabilities are short-term obligations and debts due to outside parties; the usual definition of a 'current' liability is that of being due within one year. The finance managers, however, will almost certainly want to assess the impact of other near-term liabilities which are due up to, say, two years later. Typical components of current liabilities include:

(*a*) *Trade creditors*. This forms a very short-term source of finance – probably no longer than two months in most cases.

(*b*) *Accrued expenses*. These are creditors for various services, i.e. rent, rates, wages. In published Profit and Loss Accounts they are often grouped with trade creditors and simply termed creditors.

(*c*) *Bank overdrafts*. Although in many cases banks allow an overdraft limit to exist for a number of years, there is no legal obligation for them to continue to do so. Thus, overdrafts have to be considered as short-term liabilities. In appraising the working-capital position, knowledge of the bank overdraft limit, the possibilities of any extensions and over what periods, will be required.

(*d*) *Bank loans*. These differ from overdrafts to the extent that there is a fixed time period for the loan. Generally, such loans will only be for short periods of time and are therefore recorded in current liabilities.

(*e*) *Proposed dividends*. The final dividend is not officially declared until the Annual General Meeting and so no cash leaves the company in respect of this until possibly six months after the year end.

(*f*) *Short-term loans*. Money can be borrowed from various banking and non-banking sources for short periods of time. There are a number of finance companies who specialise in arranging such types of finance.

(*g*) *Tax payments due.* Tax which is due for payment within one year is shown in current liabilities.

Apart from the prior items there are other near-term liabilities that may be included in working-capital analyses, one of the most common being taxation on the profits for the year. Typically, this amount will not be paid until at least one year but no more than two years after the year end. Other possible items are debentures and long-term loans which are near their date of redemption. As long-term loan capital often constitutes quite large sums of money, the impact of any redemption needs to be carefully studied.

In addition to the present current liabilities of the company, the impact of fixed expenses and fixed legal obligations needs to be monitored in managing working capital. This will especially apply if the working-capital position is poor and if there is some restriction or downturn in sales, e.g. a strike by delivery men. Examples

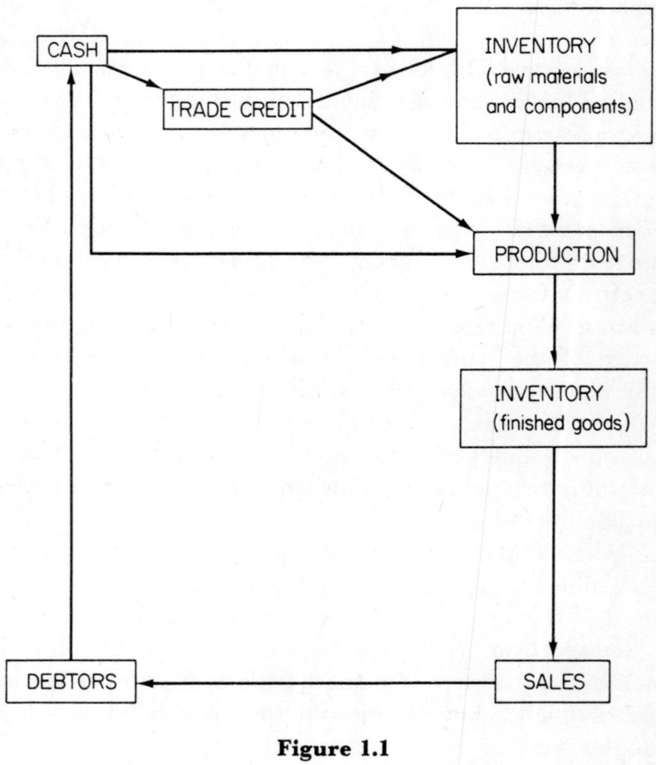

Figure 1.1

of fixed obligations include lease agreements and hire-purchase contracts.

Items (*a–d*) and (*f*) represent funds or resources supplied to the firm without them having been paid for and therefore represent sources from which increased finance can be raised if the conditions are right. Items (*e*) and (*g*), however, represent expenses which have occurred in a prior period and which have not been paid for yet (this is because accounts are drawn up using what is known as the 'accruals convention') – they do not represent funds or services supplied to the firm.

The above represent the major component items of working capital. Table 1.1 gives a typical example of where these items appear in published accounts.

The Nature of Working Capital

The nature and inter-relationships of working capital can be best described, perhaps, by the cash or operations cycle of the firm. The following example of this cycle is graphically shown in Fig. 1.1. A manufacturing firm starts with cash which it invests in raw materials and bought-in components (thus increasing inventory). Additional inventory can be bought on trade credit, thus increasing creditors. From here, further cash is expended and further trade credit obtained to enable production of finished goods, which are eventually sold on credit and hence debtors are increased. Eventually the debtors pay and the firm's cash and bank balances rise; from the cash balances the creditors are to be repaid. Adaptations can easily be made to show the cycle of retailing firms and financial firms. In the latter case, the cycle would look like:

CASH ⟶ DEBTORS ⟶ CASH

This cyclical nature of the cash flows has given rise to the term 'circulating capital'. However, the longer-term fixed assets are also part of the cash cycle, i.e.

CASH ⟶ FIXED ASSETS PURCHASED ⟶
PROFITS FROM PRODUCTION ⟶ CASH

Thus both fixed assets and working capital are strictly 'circulating capital' and therefore it can be confusing to use this description for just one of them. Working capital, however, circulates that much

Table 1.1

*Balance Sheet as at 31 December 197_*

	£	£	£
Fixed assets			10,000
Goodwill			2,000
Investments (long-term)			1,000
Current assets			
Inventory (stocks) & work in progress	2,500		
Accounts receivable (debtors)	1,500		
Prepayments*	500		
Short-term investments: quoted	500		
non-quoted	1,000		
Cash and bank balances	1,000		
		7,000	
Current liabilities			
Trade creditors	1,500		
Accrued expenses	200		
Bank overdraft†	—		
Bank loans	—		
Proposed dividend	300		
Short-term loans	1,000		
Current taxation	1,000		
		4,000	
			3,000
			£16,000
Financed by			
Share capital			4,000
Reserves			10,000
			14,000
Long-term loans			1,500
Amounts set aside for future taxation			500
			£16,000

* Includes bills receivable.

† Includes bills payable.

NOTE: the item 'Amount set aside for future taxation' represents money due to the Inland Revenue after one year but normally before two years after the balance-sheet date. It is, therefore, a near-term liability.

quicker; the speed of circulation or the 'turnover' of current assets is one indicator of its efficient management – generally the faster the better.

The level of net working capital is usually a long-term function of the sales turnover of the Company. Thus for most well-established companies the net working capital is at a near-constant ratio to sales when measured over a number of years. In the short run, however, there can be significant fluctuations in the ratio of net working capital to sales for individual companies and this especially applies if the business is seasonal. There will also be a divergence in working capital to sales ratios between different companies.

An important characteristic of working capital is its volatile nature and this imposes strains on its financing. Fig. 1.2 shows an example of the make-up of total assets for a typical firm over a period of ten years. Fixed assets tend to expand continuously over the whole period. Likewise, a significant part of the current assets increase at a fairly continuous rate (i.e. related to sales turnover as previously

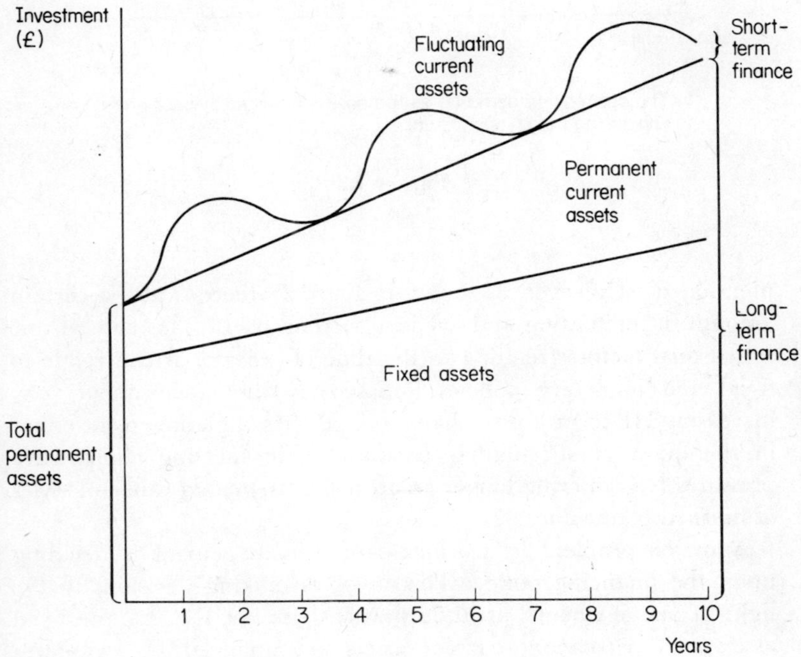

Figure 1.2

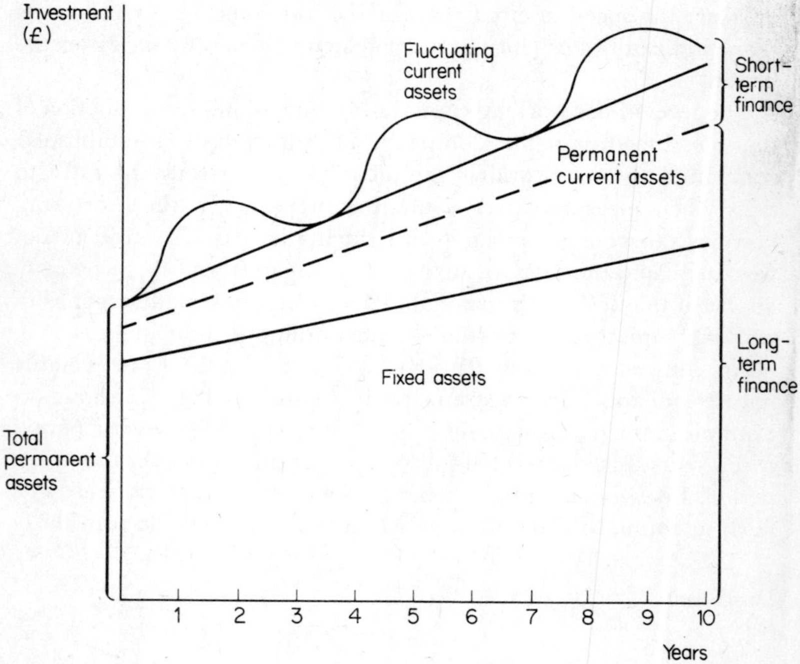

The dashed line demarcates the assets financed by short-term finance and long-term finance

Figure 1.3

mentioned). However, as shown in Fig. 1.2, there is also a certain amount of fluctuating and cyclical current assets. This can be due to seasonal factors (relating to the time of year) or it can relate to fiscal and monetary policies imposed by the Government (e.g. increasing HP terms) or to changes in policies of management either in the quest of stimulating business or in meeting competitive pressures (e.g. offering longer credit terms, increased range of styles of finished goods stocks).

A major problem in working-capital management is deciding upon the financing policy. This involves making decisions in the light of management's attitude towards risk. In Fig. 1.2 the fixed assets and permanent current assets are financed by long-term capital whilst the fluctuating current assets are financed by short-term

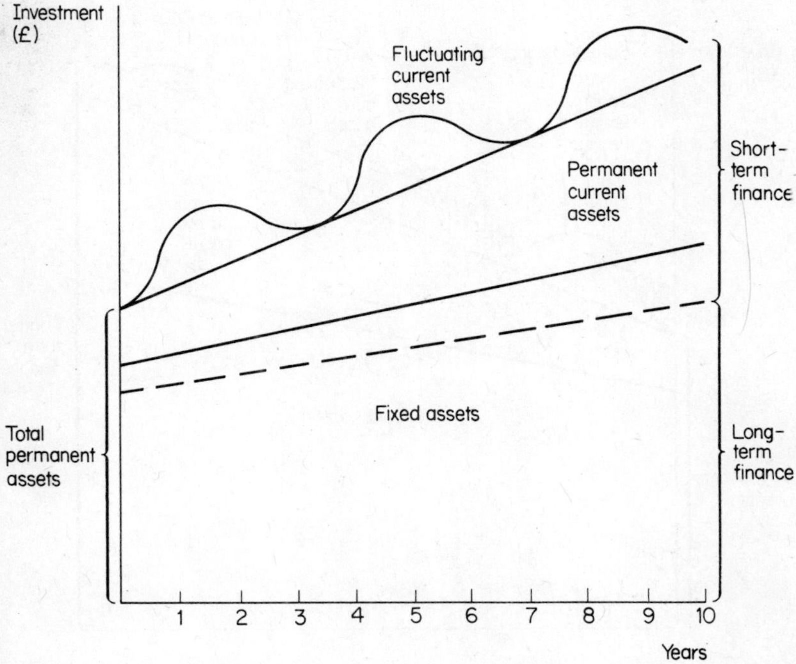

The dashed line demarcates the assets financed by short-term finance and long-term finance

Figure 1.4

credit. Thus at periods where there were no fluctuating current assets, no finance was outstanding and so no interest payable.

Alternative methods of financing current assets are shown in Figs. 1.3, 1.4 and 1.5. Fig. 1.3 shows the position where short-term finance is used to finance the fluctuating current assets and part of the permanent current assets. Fig. 1.4 shows the position where short-term finance funds the fluctuating current assets, the permanent current assets and part of the fixed assets. The last two financing strategies are more risky (and Fig. 1.4 is more risky than Fig. 1.3) as short-term finance involves uncertainty as to the interest rates and as to the availability of the finance itself. For example, if short-term finance became tight because of Government legislation (i.e. overdraft restrictions) then the company may not be able to refund its

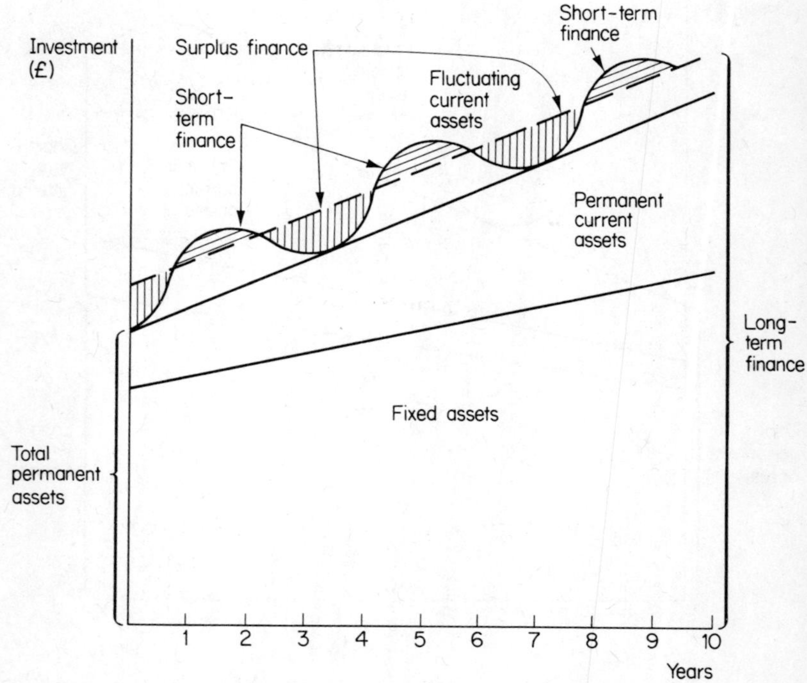

The dashed line demarcates the assets financed by short-term finance and long-term finance

Figure 1.5

short-term finance when it expires, which may well involve the bankruptcy of the firm. The advantage of using short-term finance for financing long-term assets, however, is that it often carries a lower interest rate; the financing decision therefore consists largely of a trade-off between risk and return. A more thorough discussion of the financing alternatives is given in Chapter 5.

Figure 1.5 shows the position where even the fluctuating current assets are financed by long-term capital (up to the dotted line). When the fluctuating current assets are nil, the surplus long-term finance will be invested in marketable securities pending the upsurge of current-asset investment. This strategy is the safest in terms of risk (although there is a commitment to paying interest on the loan even if it is surplus – of course, the interest on marketable securities can offset this cost) but it is often more costly. The strategy depicted in Fig. 1.5 is safest as regards risk because the dates of repayment (if any) of the principal amounts of long-term finance are known with certainty. Accordingly, new sources of finance can be planned or an orderly realisation of assets can take place. If assets were financed from short-term funds and if these sources contracted very sharply the company could be bankrupted. Although the assets cover the financing they may normally take several months to realise and if any forced sales are made a severely reduced price will probably have to be accepted. The financing of current assets, which is discussed in Chapter 5, will therefore be concerned with the liquidity structure of the assets in determining the appropriate sources of funding.

The Volume and Trends in Working Capital of British Companies

Tables 1.2, 1.3 and 1.4 give statistics and ratios relating to the working capital requirements of quoted companies in the manufacturing, distribution, construction and miscellaneous service industries. Whilst a substantial amount of net current assets are held by firms not covered by the above definition, the tables do indicate the vast resources invested in working capital (banking, finance, investment, insurance and property companies are substantially different in their financial structures from those included in the tables and so any analysis of the aggregated amounts would be spurious).

Table 1.2, extracted from the Annual Abstract of Statistics, shows a summary of the balance sheets of the population companies. Table 1.3 uses this data to compute a number of ratios to show the relative importance of working capital in the financial structure of companies. Quite clearly there has been growth in current assets as a percentage of total assets during the past eight years. After allowing for inflation, the absolute increases in current assets may look minimal but, nevertheless, the statistics still indicate substantial resources invested in these assets. Table 1.2 also shows that there has been a dramatic increase in current liabilities and this has provided an increasingly important source of funds.

The ratio statistics relating to the individual components of current assets and current liabilities are shown in Table 1.4. The only items which stand out are the lower proportions of stocks and the increased proportion of investments making up the current asset

Table 1.2

Income and finance of quoted companies[1]
(Balance sheet summary)

Balance sheet at end of 'year'[2]	1964[3]	1965	1966	1967	1968	1969	1969[4]	1970[4]	1971[4]
Number of companies	*2,283*	*2,198*	*2,109*	*1,993*	*1,829*	*1,701*	*1,366*	*1,308*	*1,239*
Fixed assets									
Tangible fixed assets, net	10,083	11,165	11,759	11,642	12,389	13,120	12,967	13,707	14,949
Goodwill	668	710	814	829	1,118	1,290	1,255	1,405	1,572
Trade investments	778	859	884	781	—	—	—	—	—
Investment in unconsolidated subsidiaries	55	110	64	65	66	92	112	153	139
Total fixed assets, etc.	11,585	12,844	13,521	13,317	13,573	14,502	14,334	15,264	16,660
Current assets:									
Stocks and work in progress	6,008	6,566	6,868	6,966	7,467	8,208	7,912	8,741	9,053
Trade and other debtors, etc.	5,147	5,695	6,167	6,622	7,500	8,362	8,148	8,948	8,759
Investments	392	308	341	610	1,533	1,487	1,543	1,702	1,980
of which: British government securities	66	47	32	42	15	14	16	13	14
Loans to local authorities	39	27	18	20	17	11	7	2	2
Other and unclassified quoted securities	218	173	224	307	778	674	690	715	799
Unquoted	69	61	67	241	723	789	830	972	1,165
Tax reserve certificates	97	46	43	61	41	29	31	30	36
Treasury bills	8	2	2	1	2	—	—	—	—
Cash	950	911	960	1,115	1,208	1,238	1,260	1,210	1,554
Total current assets	12,601	13,528	14,382	15,375	17,749	19,325	18,894	20,631	21,383

Less Current liabilities:									
Bank overdrafts and loans	1,302	1,645	1,876	1,871	2,114	2,601	2,505	3,001	2,887
Trade and other creditors, etc.	4,078	4,563	4,852	5,152	5,839	7,000	6,895	8,132	8,439
Dividends and interest due	409	445	595	597	611	622	611	621	693
Current taxation	881	734	708	749	1,709	1,859	1,868	1,688	1,594
Total current liabilities	6,669	7,387	8,031	8,369	10,273	12,082	11,879	13,441	13,614
Net current assets	5,932	6,141	6,351	7,006	7,476	7,243	7,015	7,190	7,769
Total net assets	17,516	18,985	19,872	20,323	21,049	21,745	21,349	22,454	24,430
Represented by:									
Future tax reserves	772	697	720	760	29	34	40	51	120
Long-term loans	2,276	2,622	3,158	3,635	4,150	4,355	4,443	4,767	5,250
Minority interests in subsidiaries	519	588	604	705	813	900	897	865	973
Shareholders' interest	13,949	15,078	15,389	15,223	16,057	16,456	15,969	16,771	18,085
of which: Ordinary shares	5,866	6,106	6,179	5,950	6,020	6,199	6,012	6,187	6,391
Preference, etc. shares	1,042	1,028	924	837	734	606	559	533	514
Capital and revenue reserves	6,747	7,611	7,920	8,097	8,903	9,215	8,993	9,603	10,533
Tax equalisation reserve	294	333	366	339	400	437	406	448	647
Accumulated depreciation on fixed assets	5,304	5,923	6,498	6,669	7,333	7,852	7,635	8,382	8,979
Contracts for capital expenditure not provided for	789	812	753	683	820	977	1,021	1,164	876

[1] The figures are derived from the accounts of quoted companies, engaged mainly in the United Kingdom in manufacturing, distribution, construction and certain miscellaneous services. They exclude companies whose main interests are in agriculture, shipping, insurance, banking, finance and property and those operating wholly or mainly overseas.

[2] The 'year' is, for each company included, its accounting year which ended between 6 April of the year shown and 5 April of the following year.

[3] The figures for 1964, with comparable figures for later years, are confined to quoted companies with net assets of £500,000 or more or gross income of £50,000 or more in 1964.

[4] The figures for 1970 (with comparable figures for 1969) and 1971 are confined to quoted companies with net assets of £2·0 million or more or gross income of £0·2 million or more in 1968.

Source: Department of Trade and Industry.

Table 1.3

	1964	1971
Current assets as a percentage of all assets (less accumulated depreciation)	52·0	56·2
Current assets as a percentage of all assets (gross amounts)	42·7	45·5
Current assets as a percentage of current liabilities	189	157
Current liabilities as a percentage of total financing	27·6	48·5

Table 1.4

Items as a percentage of current assets

	1964	1971
Stocks	47·4	42·3
Debtors	40·8	41·0
Investments	3·4	9·3
Tax Reserve Certificates and Treasury Bills	0·9	0·1
Cash	7·5	7·3
	100·0	100·0

Items as a percentage of current liabilities

	1964	1971
Bank overdrafts and loans	19·5	21·2
Trade and other creditors	61·1	62·0
Dividends and interest due	6·2	5·1
Current taxation	13·2	11·7
	100·0	100·0

Table 1.5

Percentage of make-up of sources of company funds

	1964	1965	1966	1967	1968	1969	1970	1971
Receipts from new issues	11·9	13·2	16·5	20·2	26·6	15·9	13·1	17·7
Increase in short-term credit	16·2	17·0	10·5	10·4	12·6	22·5	24·5	1·1
Internal sources	71·9	69·8	73·0	69·4	60·8	61·6	62·4	81·2
	100·0	100·0	100·0	100·0	100·0	100·0	100·0	100·0

total. Apart from the slight patterns in these two items there has been no major change in the component make-up of current assets and current liabilities.

Table 1.5 shows the percentage make-up of sources of company funds over the period 1964 to 1971. Short-term credit as provided by banking sources and trade and other creditors has played an important part in the financing of firms. However, this source has tended to be fairly volatile and thus companies will find it more difficult to rely on short-term credit and to forecast it. Indeed, it is possible for credit from banking and trade-credit sources to actually decrease during the year.

Table 1.6 shows the percentage make-up of the uses of funds of the population companies in the period 1964 to 1971. The table

Table 1.6

Percentage make-up of the uses of company funds

	1964	1965	1966	1967	1968	1969	1970	1971
Payments out of income	34·2	36·0	38·0	35·9	30·4	31·9	34·5	39·9
Expenditure on fixed assets	40·1	44·4	42·6	38·3	38·8	40·6	41·8	49·8
Increase in current assets	25·7	19·6	19·4	25·8	30·8	27·5	23·7	10·3
	100·0	100·0	100·0	100·0	100·0	100·0	100·0	100·0

emphasises not only the large annual increments to current assets but also the erratic nature of the increases. This high degree of variability is caused by boom–slump conditions which have prevailed during recent economic history and the impact of movements in short-term credit available to companies. When there is a sudden cutback in trade credit granted to firms, the easiest and possibly the only way for them to meet this is to reduce current assets; this, in practice, means tighter credit control of debtors and reducing inventories.

In interpreting the above tables note should be made of the following factors:

(1) they only include certain industries;

(2) they are aggregated figures and any unusual items relevant to particular companies will not be highlighted;

(3) absolute figures are used with no account of inflation being taken. Once inflation has been accounted for there may have been little expansion in working capital (i.e. physical inventory levels may have been virtually the same throughout the period).

Even allowing for the above factors, the statistics presented in Tables 1.2, 1.3, 1.4, 1.5 and 1.6 show that gross working capital represents a very substantial portion of industries' assets and that current liabilities represent an important source of finance. Additionally, the level of working capital is shown to be very variable. This is because it is liable to very sudden and very drastic cuts on the input side and because on the uses side, current assets are the most manageable (i.e. capable of being converted easily and quickly into cash).

The Management of Working Capital

As has just been discussed, substantial resources are devoted to working capital and for many companies more than half their assets are in inventories, debtors and cash. In spite of the enormous amounts involved, very little management or control of working capital was done until quite recently; often the only management was that by necessity, i.e. reducing current assets to meet overdraft requirements. However, numerous quantitative techniques have been derived and applied over recent years which have enabled a closer control to be applied to working capital.

The main advances in the application of control of working capital have come from both a greater detailed examination and analysis of the items and from the adoption of numerical 'optimisation' techniques. Examples of the first have been developed because of more skilled personnel, improved management-information systems which have allowed more detailed analyses, improvement in outside services and agencies that can be employed (i.e. debt-collection agencies) and the use of ratios. Quantitative techniques that have been applied include probabilistic forecasting and optimisation techniques (i.e. techniques which give an 'optimal' answer given the data input); for example, the general inventory model sets out to optimise the 'costs' of holding inventory against the 'costs' of not holding inventory. These techniques are reliant on the adequacy of the management-information system and also on the availability of computing time.

On the financing side of current assets there have been numerous developments in recent years. This has involved an increased number of financing alternatives, for example, leasing equipment and factoring of debts, and each has its own 'risk' characteristics. Whilst the increased number of financing alternatives available is beneficial to companies, it has also required a greater sophistication in deciding between the sources. Thus, much greater detailed analysis and care is needed in managing the financing of current assets.

Without any management the working-capital position can become quite serious and the major consequences of such conditions are given in the next section. The reason for working capital not being able to 'optimise' itself is that there are various functional areas influencing it, and these primarily look after their own needs. For example, the production department will be wanting high stocks of raw materials so there will be no hold-up of the production process whatsoever; the marketing function will desire high levels of finished stocks to immediately satisfy customer requirements and they will also desire long credit terms, again to satisfy customers. These 'high' stocks and debtors levels require heavy financing charges which the functional managers may not be aware of, or care about. Therefore, there needs to be some overall control of working capital so as to optimise the firm's overall objectives. Such overall responsibility often rests in the financial management or corporate planning department of the company as their personnel are possibly in the best position to measure the overall impact of various policies. Thus the control of working capital rests with many functional areas of management, although some central decision-making will be required to optimise the total effort, involving contributions from all the various functional managers so that 'optimal' policies can be pursued.

THE BENEFITS FROM MANAGING WORKING CAPITAL

Having established that techniques do exist for the management and control of working capital it is now necessary to recognise the nature of the benefits that may accrue from applying them. The items below cover the major ramifications of poor working-capital management:

(1) The cost of holding current assets. Inventories and debtors are idle assets and do not generally attract interest. There is therefore a cost of holding these assets representing the interest foregone that could have been earned on cash. Thus, other things being equal, inventories and debtors should be reduced to nil balances; other things are not equal, however, and management has to 'optimise' between the cost of holding these assets and other factors. Poor control of inventory and debtors can also result in losses through not recognising the holding of obsolete lines of stock and bad debts.

(2) The 'cost' of having no working capital. One example is having a low level of inventory such that customer requirements cannot be met. Not only does this result in lower-than-potential sales for the period but it may force customers to look elsewhere for their longer-term requirements. Sales may also be lost if the company is unable to provide competitive credit terms to customers (through a lack of cash or poor management insight of credit policies to adopt).

(3) The inability to meet debts when they become due. This will lead to technical insolvency and eventually to liquidation; thus the very existence of the firm is threatened. (Legal insolvency is defined as being unable to pay your debts even when all the assets are realised; technical insolvency is slightly less serious, representing the position when the company does not have time to realise its assets so as to pay its creditors.) Whilst companies generally become insolvent because of poor trading performance, there have also been a surprising number of spectacular company crashes when the firm has

been operating 'successfully'; in such cases it is nearly always the result of inadequate attention being given to working capital.

An additional factor is that governments in the recent past have at various times drastically curbed money supply such that short-term financing becomes extremely tight. Thus a company with low net working capital could be in a serious liquidity plight, if the government adopts a sudden and strong deflationary strategy; likewise, any large increase in short-term interest rates will severely hit companies which rely heavily on short-term finance.

An example of a fast expanding company being forced into liquidation through inadequate working capital is given below.

The Excel Company sells a very popular brand of convenience foods through its twenty retail outlets. The food pack costs 80p to buy and it sells to the public at 100p. Excel followed a policy of keeping an anticipated thirty-day supply of food packs in stock – this represents the expected sales in the succeeding month. The marketing department predicted an increase in sales of 5000 packs each month beginning in June. The company's customers pay their debts on the first day of the month following the month of sale and Excel pays its own creditors as they become due. The operating costs (i.e. wages, rent and rates) come to £3000 per month and are paid when due. Table 1.7 shows the financial position as at 1 April; this consisted of £20,000 in cash, £16,000 in inventory and £20,000 in accounts receivable; it then goes on to show the performance of the company during the next six months (the forecast sales were exactly achieved).

The table shows both the accounting profits of the company (prepared on the normal accruals basis) and the cash flow. By the end of August the company's bank balance was reduced to nothing and, in the absence of banking support, Excel would be unable to pay its bills in September – this of course will eventually lead to its creditors petitioning for the winding up of the company. During the period covered, the requirements for increased investments in inventory and accounts receivable were so demanding because of the rapid growth of sales that all the available cash (from both the opening balance and that generated from debtors) was unable to meet Excel's requirements – this being in spite of the company's good accounting profits position.

Whilst the Excel situation is quite simple to understand, many financial managers in fact fail to recognise the problem in their own

Table 1.7

	April (£)	May (£)	June (£)	July (£)	August (£)	September (£)
1. CASH at the beginning of the month	20,000	21,000	18,000	11,000	5,000	—
2. ACCOUNTS RECEIVABLE at 1st of the month (equal to previous month's sales)	20,000	20,000	20,000	25,000	30,000	35,000
3. INVENTORY at the end of the month UNITS (equals forecast unit sales of next month)	20,000	25,000	30,000	35,000	40,000	45,000
£ VALUE (80p per pack)	16,000	20,000	24,000	28,000	32,000	36,000
4. SALES: UNITS	20,000	20,000	25,000	30,000	35,000	40,000
£ Value	20,000	20,000	25,000	30,000	35,000	40,000
5. COST OF SALES (80p per unit pack sold)	16,000	16,000	20,000	24,000	28,000	32,000
6. OPERATING COSTS	3,000	3,000	3,000	3,000	3,000	3,000
7. MONTHLY ACCOUNTING PROFITS (4 − (5 + 6))	1,000	1,000	2,000	3,000	4,000	5,000
8. CUMULATIVE ACCOUNTING PROFITS	1,000	2,000	4,000	7,000	11,000	16,000
CASH FLOW						
Cash on Hand	20,000	21,000	18,000	11,000	5,000	—
Cash received from debtors (i.e. previous month's sales)	20,000	20,000	20,000	25,000	30,000	35,000
	40,000	41,000	38,000	36,000	35,000	35,000
Cash payments: purchases:	16,000	20,000	24,000	28,000	32,000	36,000
operating costs:	3,000	3,000	3,000	3,000	3,000	3,000
	19,000	23,000	27,000	31,000	35,000	39,000
CLOSING CASH BALANCE	21,000	18,000	11,000	5,000	—	−4,000

organisations (i.e. that a rapid growth in a company results in a necessity for substantial additional financing to maintain liquidity) and this has led to a number of recent failures of 'quite successful' companies.

If the situation had been recognised then remedial action could have been taken. This may have consisted of (*a*) obtaining additional longer-term financing in plenty of time; (*b*) arranging credit from suppliers and banks; (*c*) restructuring the selling prices; it would appear from Table 1.7 that the product is very successful and that possibly a higher price could be charged; (*d*) a shortening of the period of credit could be made; again as the product is successful little loss of custom may arise; and (*e*) inventory levels could be cut.

Shortage of cash to meet debts can also occur due to the poor control of other current assets. For example, a firm may reasonably rely on a quick sale of its inventories or the sale of its debtors to a factoring company (described in Chapter 5) to meet any sudden or seasonal demand for cash. If, however, these assets have been poorly controlled they may not realise sufficient cash. For example the inventory may be obsolete and the debtors may be bad; these circumstances have lead to a number of company bankruptcies.

(4) Whilst maintaining solvency is the major requirement of working-capital management the firm will also find it has to show some premium over this level if it is to keep credibility with the outside world. Thus, trade creditors, bankers, fixed-interest investors and equity investors will all be analysing the firm as to its credit-worthiness: If they think there is a significant chance of future insolvency then they are unlikely to deal with the company or at least to deal with the company on such good terms.

Management will therefore find it 'pays' to keep working-capital positions within certain limits. This will generally mean keeping above certain minimum ratios – ratio analysis is probably the major yardstick used by creditors, bankers and fixed-interest investors in their appraisal of creditworthiness. This 'confidence' factor is therefore an additional factor that has to be considered in working-capital management.

The Aim of the Book

Modern financial management recognises that the various resources of the firm are highly interwoven and dependent upon each other.

This means that before any decisions are taken on individual items, the impact on the business as a whole must be ascertained and considered. Thus, to consider any one part of the firm's resources alone, such as working capital, is artificial and can lead to suboptimal results. In understanding the integrated whole, however, one will need knowledge of the parts. This especially applies in management education where major items such as working capital need to be studied separately in order to make the subject tenable. The purpose of this book is to describe methods and analytical techniques for managing working capital; this will involve a discussion of the working-capital situation and its relationship to the business environment as well as a description of numerical optimisation techniques.

The literature on the management of working capital has been quite sparse; this is in stark contrast to the literature on the analysis of fixed assets (capital-expenditure decisions) where there are any number of books in existence. Most of the conceptual theory and analytical techniques relating to working capital have appeared in academic journals and have referred to just one component item of working capital. This book sets out to fill the gap and present an overall review of the management of working capital.

The book is intended as a comprehensive text for first- and second-year undergraduates in accountancy and business studies; it will also be useful for the major professional qualifications in these subjects. Whilst the management of working capital is carried out by various functional managers as previously described, the book is aimed primarily at the overall control or financial control of working capital. Thus there is no in-depth study of inventory control which, in the case of raw materials and work-in-progress, may rest largely with the production department. In the light of the intended audience, the book has been approached from both a conceptual and a practical application viewpoint. No great mathematical knowledge is required in reading the text although relevant models and quantitative techniques are introduced during the course of the book. The references given at the end of each chapter give more specialised reading on individual topics, although the book in itself represents a full text for the audience aimed at.

CONTENTS

The analysis and control of the major components of current assets, viz. inventories, debtors and cash, are set out in separate chapters

(Chapters 2, 3 and 4) because the items are sufficiently different as to obviate the use of a common approach. Each chapter covers the description, problem situations, analyses and optimisation techniques relevant to the assets concerned. For example, inventories can come in various forms (i.e. raw materials, work-in-progress); they are to be managed with a view to providing customer service as well as to keeping the cost down (these generally being incompatible); various ratios can provide yardsticks for control; and quantitative methods exist to give 'optimal' inventory levels. Chapter 5 gives a description of the major sources of short-term finance available to companies. Following from this, Chapter 6 discusses the analysis of working-capital positions by outside parties – this is used by management in determining credit facilities to offer to individual clients and in anticipating creditor reactions to their own working-capital position. Finally, Chapter 7 introduces various short-term forecasting techniques which are applicable to sales and working-capital forecasts.

CHAPTER 2

Inventory Management

For the manufacturing and distributive trades, inventories (or stocks) constitute a substantial portion of the total assets employed and, as will be seen, a good deal of control and management can be applied to them. Inventories can be broken down into the following types:

Raw materials and bought-in components. These represent stocks held by manufacturing industries prior to their being utilised in the production process.

Work-in-progress. This is the term given to a product which is only part-way through a manufacturing process. It consists of raw materials and bought-in components, labour costs, subcontracting costs and various manufacturing costs.

Finished goods. These are the products that the company sells to its customers. In the case of the distributive industry, finished goods are likely to be the only type of inventory.

Reasons for Holding Stocks

The purpose of good stock control is to balance the costs of holding stocks against the benefits derived from doing so. (Costs of holding stocks represent the expenses involved with keeping items in stock; this does not include the purchase price of the goods.) Whilst recognising and measuring the costs requires a good deal of analysis, the benefits from holding stocks are fairly obvious and are set out below.

Raw materials and bought-in components: (*a*) to provide a safety stock against a failure of supplies for any reason. This is especially important in a continuous manufacturing process where large fixed costs are involved and for industries which have sales contracts with fixed-date completions. Examples of the first include the automobile industry, chemical processes and metal refining; (*b*) to allow the purchasing department to take advantage of lower prices, which may occur through bulk purchasing or because of a special offer or a temporary recession in prices (i.e. seasonal products). Additionally, if large price increases are forecast then a large bulk purchase may be made at the current prevailing prices; (*c*) to minimise the administrative costs that are involved each time a purchase is made.

Work-in-progress: (*a*) to act as a safety stock of raw materials. If a process involves going from one production shop to another, then a stoppage in the first because of an industrial dispute, machine breakdown or any other reason, will cause the second to shut down. By holding safety stocks some protection is given against the whole factory becoming idle. Thus continuous production runs are made more certain in the various subassemblies or subprocesses in the factory; (*b*) In some processes there may be a number of variants of the final product. In such cases an inventory of partially finished goods can be kept and these are completed as and when a specific customer order comes in. This could apply to an exclusive range of cars where the basic chassis of the vehicle is kept in stock and the trimmings, colour etc. applied when a sale contract is signed.

Finished goods: (*a*) to provide customer service. If there are stock shortages then sales will be lost. (*b*) to allow continuous production runs even if sales are seasonal. For example, greetings-card manufacturers will build up finished stocks of Christmas cards from, say, June onwards, not because of customer requirements but in order to allow a continuous production run on the existing printing machines.

Costs Involved with Holding Stocks

The costs associated with stocks can be classified into the following groupings:

(1) The holding costs which represent the expenses of holding the goods in stock.

(2) Procurement expenses which are incurred each time a purchase order has to be made.

(3) The 'costs' of running short of inventory (stock-out costs).

These items are not as obvious as many other types of costs and careful analysis is required. Additionally, the items are dependent very largely on the stockholding policies of the company and thus on management decisions. These items of costs will be discussed below.

COST OF HOLDING STOCKS (CARRYING COSTS)

There are numerous costs associated with holding goods in stock. The major expense is the 'interest forgone' or 'interest paid' on the cash tied up in stocks. In buying stocks, the firm has to pay out cash on which it could otherwise have earned interest (or invested in an asset which produces a return); alternatively, it may have had to pay interest on an overdraft. This 'interest forgone' or 'interest paid' is a very real cost to the business and must be accounted for as management has control over the level of stocks to hold and hence control over the 'interest forgone' (or, in economic terminology, the 'opportunity cost').

Other expenses of holding stocks are perhaps more obvious. Amongst the more common items are extra storage costs involved (the opportunity cost), insurance, damage, deterioration, pilferage, obsolescence and the administrative costs in keeping stock records.

The above expenses represent varying values in different businesses and trades although they are all approximately proportional to the value of the stocks and to the length of time for which they are held. The table below gives a representative summary of the costs of holding stocks in industry as a percentage of the cost price of the stocks:

	(per cent p.a.)
Interest or cost of money tied up	15*
Storage	3
Damage, deterioration and pilferage	2
Obsolescence	5
Insurance	1
	26% p.a.

*1975

This is an average figure; most companies come within the range 20 to 30 per cent per annum; additionally, this cost is before taxation and so it acts to reduce the tax charge. Until the present high level of interest rates began in 1973, the cost of money tied up was more in the region of 10 per cent. This rate of interest is in relation to the cost of borrowing or lending; some arguments have been put forward for using other 'opportunity costs'. For an example see Stancill,[1] pp. 94–5.

The above costs are in terms of one year and when multiplied by the average level of stocks gives the annual charge – clearly the cost of holding stocks are very substantial. In the last few years there has been a substantial amount of inflation which has increased the interest rates; it has also, however, sent selling prices up and so, by holding stocks, increased profits have been made. Up to 1975 there had been no general analysis of the amounts of 'stock profits' made by various companies and various trades, but these are quite likely to have been substantial for the holding of many types of raw materials, commodities and even finished goods. Stock profits are something that management will have to consider in its inventory policies, although this will probably be at a subjective level.

PROCUREMENT COSTS (ORDERING COSTS)

Initially, this includes the costs involved in finding a suitable supplier of stocks. Once a good supplier relationship has been established the cost of succeeding repeat orders has to be taken into account. Not only does this include the administrative paper work in ordering goods but also the physical work involved in unloading, inspecting and storing the goods. It is probably the latter physical items which prove to be the most costly and for frequent deliveries these costs are quite high.

THE COST OF BEING OUT OF STOCK

If the firm runs out of stocks this will (*a*) result in lost sales and therefore profits in the case of finished goods, and (*b*) result in shut-downs in factory assembly lines and processes in the case of raw materials, thus causing lost production. The 'cost' is that of the lost profits (this should also take some subjective account of long-term goodwill being lost). In some cases the stock-out can be relieved by buying substitute goods, by buying components or products from outside suppliers or by special expediting (i.e. progress chasers); in this case the 'cost' is the extra cost of buying-in or the expenses of expediting (e.g. stopping everything to concentrate on the stock-out position). If the company is committed to a contract and penalty payments have to be made for late or non-delivery, then these are also costs of being out of stock. Any additional costs for meeting these back-orders will also be responsible to the stock-out.

The Need for Control of Stocks

We have just described the benefits and costs from holding stocks and we now need to explain some of the major reasons for controlling them. There are two major reasons, one being the provision of management information for the various users of stocks and, second, to optimise the benefits–costs of holding stocks.

Management information on stocks is required by the production department so that they can schedule workloads, shift-work and machine usage. For example, they require detailed knowledge of the materials and components by individual type in stock; they also need information on the work in progress, i.e. the exact state of stocks at each subassembly. This information may lead the production manager to request more purchases, revise work schedules, buy-in components or half-finished goods from suppliers and to revise budget forecasts.

Information on finished stocks is required by the marketing department so that they can estimate whether customer requirements can be met. Such data might lead the marketing manager to alter advertising and promotional campaigns, revise stock policies at retail outlets and to buy in finished goods from a competitor. Some general rules relating to management-information systems is given later.

A tight control on stocks is also needed in order to optimise the benefits–costs of holding stocks. Thus, as stock levels increase the greater the protection afforded to the production processes and the greater the ability to meet customer requirements; at the same time, however, the greater the stock levels the greater the costs. The cost–benefits are shown in Fig. 2.1 and clearly they are incompatible; therefore, management has to set off the benefits against the costs. There exist a number of decision models which the firm can use to optimise the solution and these are described in a later section.

The decisions emanating from the benefits–costs analysis are:

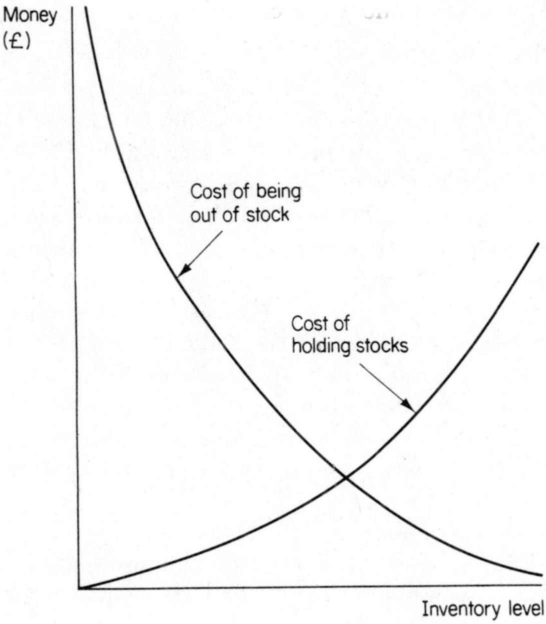

Figure 2.1

(1) What is the optimum level of stock for each item?
(2) What is the amount to re-order?
(3) When should we re-order?
(4) How often is it allowable to be out of stock?
(5) Can goods be held in a near-finished state and turned into a number of finished saleable products by a simple process upon receiving a customer order?

Without some formal control over the levels of stocks it is unlikely that the optimum level would prevail. This is because both the production department and the marketing management in carrying out their functional responsibilities will desire high inventory levels. It is for this reason that the setting of inventory policies sometimes rests with general or financial management, i.e. they have no functional bias but instead concentrate on profits and efficiency.

The main purposes of stock management are therefore to optimise stock levels and re-ordering policies and to record and control the stocks already owned.

ECONOMIC IMPLICATIONS

Quite apart from its impact on individual company performance, stock control can help even out boom-slump conditions that have prevailed in the Western World's economies for most of the century. Business or trade cycles are partially generated by the stockholding policies of corporations who alter stock levels to reflect their opinions of short-term demand. When sales demand falls, companies cut inventory levels by proportionately greater amounts and hence production is curtailed even more sharply; this produces a recession. When sales start to increase and business becomes more profitable then management desire higher levels of stocks and hence production increases at a more rapid rate; this produces boom conditions. This process hits the capital-goods industries the hardest (and hence the capital-goods cycle) as they produce the physical asset expansion for the rest of industry; any general trends in industry are magnified in capital-goods manufacturers.

With better management of stocks, better forecasting of demand and more efficient monitoring of stocks the adjustments to stocks and production can be much smoother. This will help stabilise economic development and will allow greater control over the economic environment than would otherwise have been the case.

Control of Stocks – Management Information

This section will briefly describe the recording of stocks, that is the management of goods already owned by the firm. A full description of the control techniques is not given here as the subject is very extensive, warranting a book in its own right[2,3,1] and because it is a function largely carried out by the stores department or the production department.

Although to record every individual type of stock and to record every stage of work in progress gives the maximum information, firms will generally classify stocks into certain aggregate types. This will be for two good reasons: firstly, to cut down the administrative cost and, secondly, in order to make the decision-making process more tenable (for the decision models discussed later on 'correct solutions' can still be achieved if certain items of stocks are grouped together). However, the exact aggregation of stocks has to be handled with care as too many groupings will provide much poorer information and make various decision rules suboptimum, and too few groupings takes away the advantages of aggregation.

Stocks can first of all be grouped by purpose, e.g. raw materials, bought-in components, work-in-progress and finished stocks. This will give some immediate delineation of management information; for example, the production managers will be interested in the first three categories whilst the marketing department will be primarily interested in the last.

Within these categories further breakdowns will be required and these can be specified by the various users of stocks. The production department will be concerned to have information on the stock levels of materials for which there are no substitutes, components which prevent an item continuing through a production process, or goods which take a long time to be delivered (i.e. those purchased from abroad or those that have to be custom built). Work-in-progress could be broken down by the stage of production or the areas of the factory or assembly line where the goods are held or made; that which has been subcontracted out needs special control attention. Finished stocks could be classified by major different types, by market outlets, by geographical analysis (i.e. home, export, and town and city locations for retail outlets). Further classifications within the above groupings can be made; for example, the stocks could be classified by: (*a*) the level of sales (i.e. grouping together finished stocks of slow-selling items); (*b*) the length and technical nature of the production process; and (*c*) the durability and perishability of the items (for example, fairly close control of fresh foodstuffs is required as significant losses can occur through deterioration).

CODING AND RECORDING STOCKS

In order to give an efficient management-information service each individual item of stock needs to be identified, coded and stored. Examples of coding include numerical sequencing and picture-coding systems in which certain positions within the code carry specific details of the stock; examples of picture coding that are in current use include the 'Brisch'[5] and the 'Opitz'[6] systems. Careful attention has to be given to coding systems as any alterations to the system, so as to incorporate new types of stock, can be extremely expensive. For firms with large stocks of many types, a computer will probably be found necessary in order to cope with the work and thus any coding classification needs even more careful preparation.

There are a number of ways of recording the movements of stocks although most rely on the keeping of a stock card which will show details of part numbers, replenishments, usage, dates, locations and the appropriate authorisations; it can also show the re-order dates, review periods, budget forecasts and other details. Some companies have in fact computerised the records, and analyses of the data are automatically produced giving information, for example, on purchasing requirements and customer demands. Such systems have also been installed where stock levels at retail outlets are fed to a centralised computer base.

LEVEL OF CONTROL REQUIRED

In many firms it will be found that they have stocks which are used or 'turned over' at very different rates. For example, it is often found that a small proportion of all items (say 20 per cent) will account for a large proportion (say 80 per cent) of the total usage value (i.e. the cost of a unit multiplied by the quantity used per period). Such stock-usage patterns have been described under various headings including 'distribution by value', 'A–B–C rule', 'Pareto principle' and the '80–20 rule'; an example of the pattern is shown in Fig. 2.2. This is constructed by listing the items in descending order of usage value and plotting the accumulated usage value against the number of items considered, taken as a percentage.

From the figure it can be seen that there are comparatively few items in A but they make up a large proportion of the total usage value; B items are in the intermediate range and C items are the many low-usage value items (possibly spares for old-established products). Examples of typical values are

A items make up 20 per cent of items, but 80 per cent of ottal usage value

B items make up 30 per cent of items, but 15 per cent of total usage value

C items make up 50 per cent of items, but 5 per cent of total usage value

The purpose behind the 'distribution by value' analysis is that it indicates the degree of control that is required; as the control of stocks is an expensive operation no over-sophisticated system will be warranted. For example, items A in Fig. 2.2 will require tight control because they represent a large percentage of total expenditure and because the frequency of activity gives more scope for error and fraud; items B will require lesser control and items C perhaps only slight surveillance (items C mainly requiring control for pilferage and for obsolescence reasons).

The A–B–C items are, of course, arbitrary cut-off points and management could think of others; additionally, a greater number of divisions could also be made, i.e. A, B, C, D, E. By constructing a

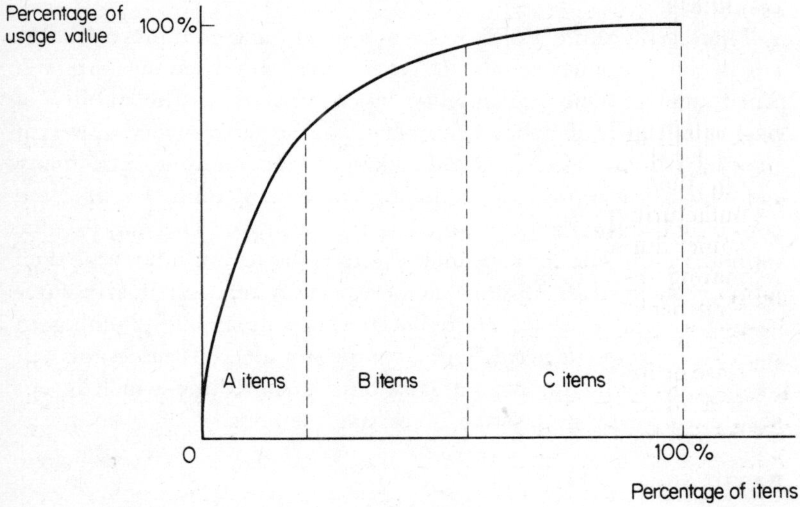

Figure 2.2

curve as in Fig. 2.2 management can determine the distribution by value classification.

FORECASTING

Stocks are held with a view to supplying future demand and therefore some forecast, whether objectively or subjectively derived, has to be made. Thus management will require an estimate of the near-future sales demand (possibly up to six months hence), and for each sub-period (in case demand is seasonal, growing or declining). As the future is uncertain, the forecast should preferably include a range of outcomes with attached probabilities. Various breakdowns of the sales forecast can be made such as geographical location in the case of retail outlets (i.e. although sales may be forecast to increase by 10 per cent this may accrue in just one part of the country; finished stock policies must therefore be adjusted accordingly).

From the forecast of sales the demands on stocks can be estimated and new stockholding policies adopted. This might involve new total finished-goods stocks, changes in the type of finished-goods stocks and possibly re-location of them. From the sales forecast and the finished-stocks policy, the raw-material stocks and work-in-progress levels can be optimised to take account of the expected conditions.

There are a number of short-term forecasting techniques available which can be applied to sales and these are summarised in Chapter 7. The extent of their applicability depends partly on the stability of past sales data – if it has been very volatile for no very apparent reason then any forecasting is likely to be tenuous. For many manufacturing industries producing component items for, say, the consumer durables industry, the best forecasting process may involve estimating the sales of consumer durables by its customer and then jobbing backwards. Another factor especially relevant in sales forecasting is that of price elasticity. If the company is planning to increase or lower its prices or if a competitor alters its prices this can have a dramatic impact on sales and is something which is not accounted for by time-series forecasting methods.

RATIO ANALYSIS

Before describing decision models that can be applied to stocks, a brief discussion of ratio analysis is required. The use of ratios is easily understood by all members of management and the results can give guidelines for control. The advantages of ratio analysis are that given the data they are easy to work out and they give yardsticks of performance; any unusual or unexpected trend in a ratio acts as a signal for management to investigate the causes. This in turn may indicate poor performance and management can take remedial action.

One commonly used ratio is the number of days stock on hand and this is given by the expression

$$\frac{\text{stock}}{\text{cost of sales for year}} \times 365$$

Thus, if the stock on hand is £20,000 and the cost of sales for the year is £120,000, then the average time for an item to be kept in stock before being sold is 61 days. Instead of expressing stock in terms of time, it can be shown in the form of stock turnover, i.e.

$$\frac{\text{cost of sales for year}}{\text{stock}}$$

In this method a period of one year is normally taken, although other periods could be used. In the example above the stock turnover works out to be 6.

In the above ratios, it is the cost of sales which is used and not the sales figure – this is because stocks are valued at cost and so therefore should be the physical sales.

In using the ratios, management should take account of the following (Chapter 6 also covers the subject of ratio analysis fairly extensively):

(1) The ratios should be computed for each individual item or each closely knit category of stock. Using aggregate ratios of raw materials, work-in-progress and all varieties of finished goods gives very poor and, very probably, misleading information.

(2) In seasonal businesses where the stock levels fluctuate greatly according to the date in the year, management should acknowledge this. For example, fireworks manufacturers are likely to have enormous stocks at, say, 30 September and virtually no stocks at 30 November; in such cases, management can compute an average ratio if the trade is mildly seasonal. However, in other more volatile cases the best procedure is to compute the ratios for different times of the year and compare them against similar dates in prior years.

(3) The number of days/stock ratio should not necessarily be taken as the number of days for which sales can be satisfied from current stocks. This is because sales may be seasonal (i.e. umbrellas, skiing equipment) and thus management must take into account that at some periods of the year stocks have to be built up to high levels, e.g. the fireworks manufacturer may show a stock turnover of 1 in, say, August or September.

(4) Trends or comparisons of ratios should be computed. For example, a stock turnover of 12 is only either good or bad when measured against some yardstick such as the ratio in prior years or periods or against other companies. If any trend has taken an

unexpected direction or reached an unexpected level, then the reasons for this should be investigated.

(5) Very great care should be exercised in using inter-company ratios, especially those with different year ends (and even more care should be taken if the business is seasonal – indeed, inter-company ratios may be quite useless in this case). Other difficulties include not knowing the accounting policies of other companies and their impact on stock valuations and that only aggregate data is likely to be available on competitors (there are a number of acceptable ways of valuing stocks and the results between these methods can vary very sharply).

There are numerous other ratios that can be computed although the two mentioned above are the most common; if management thinks that any other ratio will be useful then they should use it but at the same time be aware of the caveats expressed above. Although ratios are not as sophisticated as inventory decision models they can provide, if used at a detailed level, useful yardsticks and guidelines for managerial control.

Management may also want to compute the aggregate ratios in order to anticipate outsiders' reactions to the accounts. Shareholders, potential investors and creditors all use the annual accounts to appraise the company and the inventory ratios are likely to be amongst their analyses. By anticipating outside reaction the company may be able to ameliorate any adverse comments if the ratios appear 'bad', by issuing various explanations. Chapter 6 deals more fully with investor and creditor confidence in relation to ratios.

INVENTORY DECISION MODELS

The two main decisions that have to be made by management are what amounts of stock should be ordered and how often to make an order. The basic model discussed in this section gives 'optimum' solutions to these questions, that is 'optimum' given accurate data input. Later, derivatives of the basic model will be briefly described; these more sophisticated models allow many real-world problem situations to be incorporated in the decision analysis.

Fig. 2.3 shows the basic inventory process. Here the amount Q is ordered and this is all used up at a constant rate over the period T; at the point P the quantity Q is re-ordered and the process starts off again. Fig. 2.3 represents a very simplified situation and assumes that

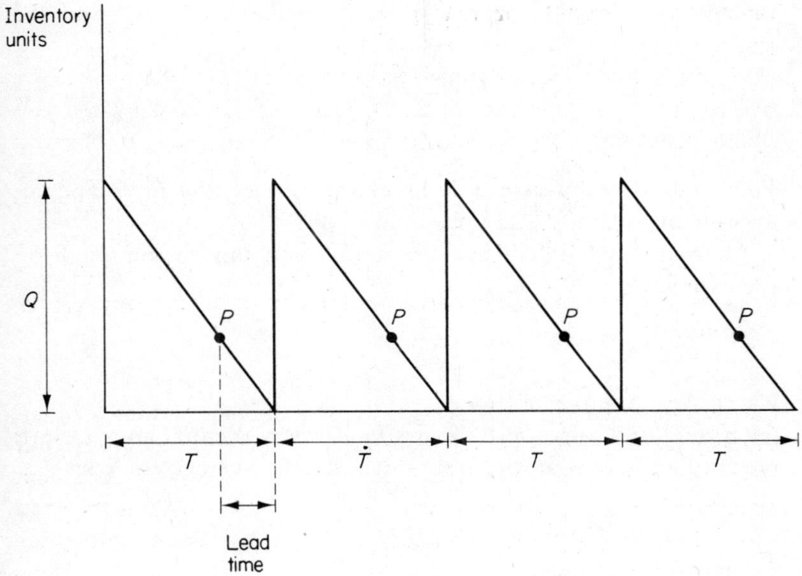

Figure 2.3

the variables are known with certainty, that demand is constant over time and that replenishment of stocks takes an exact known time. The above assumptions can be relaxed in probabilistic models and by using safety or buffer stocks; these are described later.

Using the basic inventory process of Fig. 2.3, we can see that the average inventory per period T is $\frac{1}{2}Q$, Q being the order quantity. For example, Alpha Ltd, with no opening stocks, places one order for 1000 units at the beginning of the year; no further orders are placed and the closing inventory is nil. The average stock (A) is thus

$$\begin{aligned} A &= \frac{Q}{2} \\ &= \frac{1000}{2} \\ &= 500 \text{ units.} \end{aligned}$$

If Alpha placed two orders for 500 units each (the second order being received when the first is exhausted) the average inventory would be

$$A = \frac{Q}{2}$$
$$= \frac{500}{2}$$
$$= 250 \text{ units}$$

Four orders would give a re-order amount of 250 units and an average inventory of 125 units, and so on.

Alternatively, Alpha's average stock levels can be computed by the expression

$$A = \frac{S}{2N}$$

where N = number of orders,
i.e. if total unit sales are 1000 and four orders of equal amounts are received each year at quarterly intervals, the average stock level is

$$A = \frac{S}{2N}$$
$$= \frac{1000}{8}$$
$$= 125 \text{ units}$$

Clearly, by ordering more frequently Alpha can reduce the average inventory held to smaller and smaller amounts. As described earlier in the chapter, the costs of holding stocks are quite significant and so, other things being equal, average stocks should be reduced to as low a level as possible. However, in ordering goods Alpha will incur various ordering or procurement costs and these, in the simple case, are fixed per order and delivery (see p. 27 for examples of these types of costs). Thus, the greater the number of orders per year the less the holding costs but the greater the order costs. These are clearly incompatible and are shown graphically in Fig. 2.4, which shows the inventory cost on the vertical axis and the number of orders per year, or other period of time, on the horizontal axis. The carrying costs are shown as a curve, *A*; the procurement costs are shown by the line *B* which could, in fact, be shown more realistically as a curve, i.e. procurement costs per unit may be reduced once a very large number of orders are made (e.g. a regular re-ordering system).

The total cost per unit is shown by the curve *C*, derived by computing the sum of the holding costs and the ordering costs. At point *X*

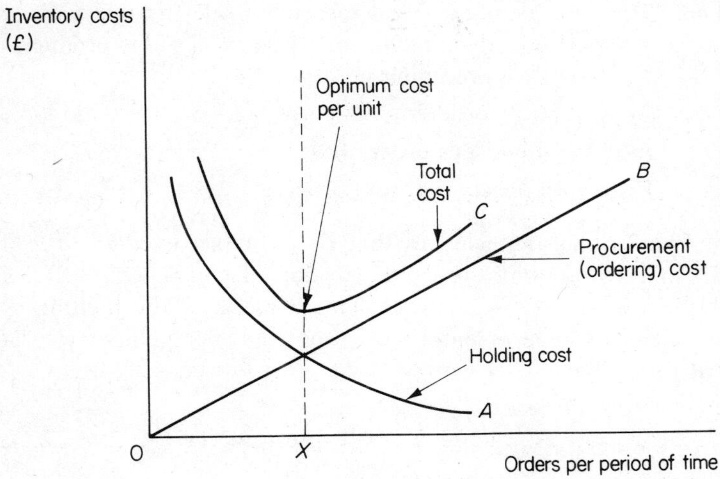

Figure 2.4

the total costs are the lowest and this also represents the minimum cost per unit. This point will be where the marginal cost of the rising expenses are equal to the marginal cost of the decreasing expenses (i.e. in Fig. 2.4 the minimum total cost is at the point where the absolute value of the slope of the rising procurement cost is equal to the absolute value of the declining holding cost). The point X tells us the number of orders we need to make during the year and hence the constant amount to order. We derive point X by in fact computing what is known as the economic order quantity (EOQ) which tells us the optimum amount to order. The derivation of the EOQ is described below (this is similar to the economic lot size (ELS) model which relates to optimum batches of production).

The Economic Order Quantity

The total cost of inventories (TC) are a function of the costs of ordering or procurement (P) and the carrying or holding costs (H), i.e. $TC = P + H$.

P, the ordering or procurement cost, is given by the expression

$$\left(\frac{F}{Q} + V\right)D$$

where D = unit demand (used instead of sales as this term can include demand of one process for the products of another preceding process),

Q = quantity ordered,

F = fixed cost per order, and

V = variable cost per unit ordered.

The expression acknowledges that the costs involved in ordering stock can include both fixed and variable elements.

H, the total carrying cost, is defined as being the holding cost per unit of average inventory, C_1, times the average inventory $\frac{1}{2}Q$. Thus total costs can be expressed as

$$TC = \left(\frac{F}{Q} + V\right)D + \tfrac{1}{2}C_1Q$$

where C_1 = holding cost per unit.

The optimum order quantity or the economic order quantity is obtained by differentiating the above expression with respect to Q, setting the derivative equal to zero, and solving for Q. Hence:

$$\frac{\partial TC}{\partial Q} = -\frac{FD}{Q^2} + \tfrac{1}{2}C_1 = 0$$

$$\tfrac{1}{2}C_1 = \frac{FD}{Q^2}$$

$$Q^2 = \frac{2FD}{C_1}$$

$$Q = \sqrt{\frac{2FD}{C_1}}$$

For example, if the carrying costs per unit are £5, the fixed cost per order is £100, the number of units demanded is 2000, and the variable cost per unit is £1, then the economic order quantity is

$$\text{EOQ} = \sqrt{\frac{2(\pounds 100)\ (2000)}{5}}$$

$$= \sqrt{\frac{400{,}000}{5}}$$

$$= \sqrt{80{,}000}$$

$$= 283 \text{ units}$$

Therefore, 283 units should be ordered every 52 days.

$$\left(\frac{\text{Units demand}}{\text{Quantity ordered}} = \frac{2000}{283} = 7{\cdot}07 \text{ orders per year} = \frac{365}{7} \text{ days} = 52{\cdot}14 \text{ days.}\right)$$

The total cost of ordering and carrying the stocks will be given by

$$TC = \left(\frac{F}{Q} + V\right) D + \tfrac{1}{2} C_1 Q$$

$$= \left(\frac{£100}{283} + £1\right) 2000 + \frac{£5 \times 283}{2}$$

$$= £2706{\cdot}7 + £707{\cdot}5$$

$$= £3414{\cdot}2$$

This will be found to be the lowest possible total cost.

Once we have established the average inventory level we can then compute the average money investment in inventory. If the purchase cost price per unit is £20, then the average amount of funds tied up is the average inventory multiplied by £20,

$$= \frac{Q}{2} \times £20$$

$$= \frac{283}{2} \times £20$$

$$= £2830$$

It must be emphasised that the above is only the basic inventory decision model; having said that, however, it is still widely used in practice (the more sophisticated derivatives are very expensive and may result in only small improvements in the solutions). In using the model, management should measure the impact of different costs for carrying and for ordering. It will be found that the EOQ and the total costs involved vary little over quite wide changes in the input assumptions; the sensitivity of the decision models will be dealt with more fully later on. In practice, the major uncertainty facing the model is the forecast unit demand; any probabilistic forecasts of demand should be used to compute a range of likely EOQs and total carrying and ordering costs (probabilistic models are briefly described later on).

Order points

In replenishing stocks, an order has to be sent out and the delivery date is at some future time. This delay in delivery is termed the lead time and is usually expressed in numbers of days; it can be very short in some cases, but for others it can be a matter of many months (e.g. custom-built machinery of a high value). It is important for the purchasing department to send out an order in sufficient time for the goods to be delivered before, or just as, existing stocks run out.

The order point is calculated as the lead time × daily usage. For example, if the daily sales or usage (if work-in-progress or raw materials) is 30 units and it takes 10 days for the supplier to deliver the goods, then an order must be sent out when the stock levels reach 300; this is shown by the point P in Fig. 2.3. If safety stocks are held then the order level should be: (lead time × daily usage) + the safety stock; if an order is placed before the receipt of goods from a prior order, then the order point becomes: (lead time × daily usage) − goods in transit.

Another method for selecting a re-order point is to select an acceptable stock-out factor which, in effect, sets a level of safety stocks to hold. The order point is found from the formula (see Snyder[7]):

$$\text{Order point} = D(L) + F\sqrt{DQ\,(L)}$$

where D = demand,
L = lead time,
F = stock-out acceptance factor, and
Q = units per order.

The stock-out factor is obtained from the probability distribution of usage which is normally assumed to Poisson distributed as in Fig. 2.5. Management must now specify a level of stock-outs it will

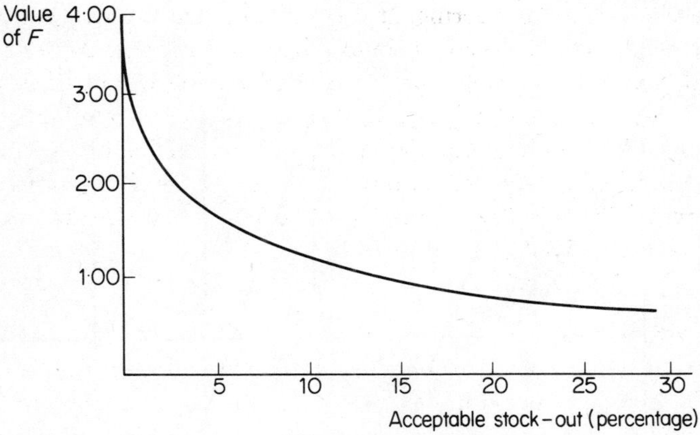

Figure 2.5

accept. The less chance it is willing to take of a stock-out the higher the F value and this will mean a higher re-order point.

For example, if $D = 200$ units per month, $L = \frac{1}{2}$ month, stock-out acceptance = 10 per cent, giving an F value of 1·29 from Fig. 2.5, and $Q = 5$, then the optimum order point is:

$$200(0{\cdot}5) + 1{\cdot}29\sqrt{(200)\ (5)\ (0{\cdot}5)} = 128{\cdot}8$$

Thus the firm should re-order when the stock level reaches 129 units, which contrasts with the general re-order level formula which gives an answer of 100 units (i.e. 200 × 0·5). The balance of 29 units represents the safety factor. This method sets an objective level of safety stocks although, in doing so, management must specify what risk of being out of stock it is prepared to accept.

Sometimes order points are taken on a regular-date basis and not on stock levels. For example, a regular review (say once a week or once a month) is made for each type of stock and action taken, usually consisting of 'topping-up' the stocks to a predetermined maximum level (i.e. the EOQ level plus any safety stock); see Fig. 2.6, and note how this contrasts with Fig. 2.8 where re-ordering is done on a re-order stock level.

Another method of ordering is the 'two bin' and 'three bin' systems. These involve putting a quantity equal to the re-order level in a separate bag or bin which is sealed or put in a separate location; the rest of the stock is withdrawn as needed with no record of individual

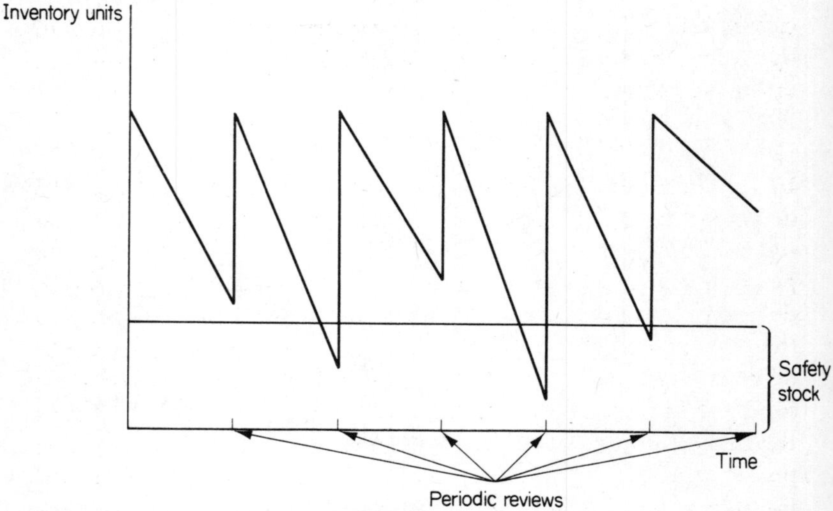

Figure 2.6

usage being kept. Opening the sealed bin, however, gives the signal for a replenishment order. This method is cheap as it does not entail continuous monitoring and is easy to understand – it has therefore gained a fair amount of acceptance. There are also other types of system in use known as the 'min–max' or 'S–s' method; these are described in the specialised inventory-control textbooks. The advantages of the review system is that it does not require a continuous monitoring of stock levels and is therefore cheaper to operate.

From the EOQ model, management will know how many times orders should be placed for stocks and they can use this information in determining review dates (taking account of seasonal biases etc.). Different review periods are likely to be applicable for different items of stock; for example, *C* items as designated in Fig. 2.2 need be reviewed far less frequently than those in the *B* and *A* categories. Because the method is not continuous there is a greater degree of uncertainty and so it is therefore most applicable (*a*) when there are safety stocks, and (*b*) when demand is fairly constant or at a known rate. Most computer systems are based on a date-review procedure.

The amount to re-order should be the economic order quantity. If there is any change expected in the rate of demand, then the amount to order should be that to bring the stocks up to the EOQ level or any revised EOQ level (which takes account of the changed circumstances). If the periodic review system of ordering stocks is in operation, then the amount to order is that which brings the stocks up to the EOQ plus any safety stock.

SAFETY STOCKS

In the inventory models just discussed we have assumed that the demand rate (the rate at which goods are sold or required at other stages of production) and the lead time for delivery are known with precision. In the real world, however, this is not the case; for example, demand could be variable, transport deliveries could be disrupted thereby increasing the time it takes a replenishment order to be delivered, or there could be a strike or production shutdown by the supplier. In such cases there could be a stock-out and this involves the 'opportunity-cost' losses as discussed on page 27. In order to protect against this a safety or 'buffer' stock can be kept. Thus, the re-order point is equal to the: (lead time $\times$ daily usage) $+$ safety stock, as described previously. If the demand and lead-time variables are known with certainty the safety-stock limit should not be broached (see Fig. 2.7). However, these variables are uncertain and

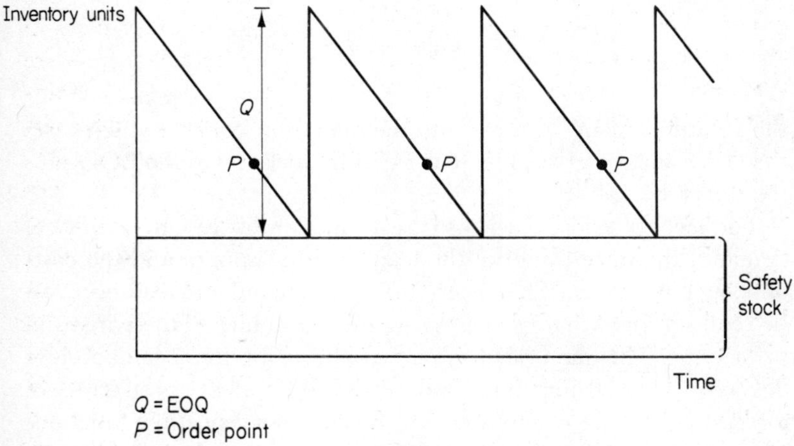

Figure 2.7

so in some instances part of the safety stocks will be used up – pictorially this is shown as in Fig. 2.8. Here the order signal is given by point *P* and it takes $4\frac{1}{2}$ time units to receive an order. As can be seen

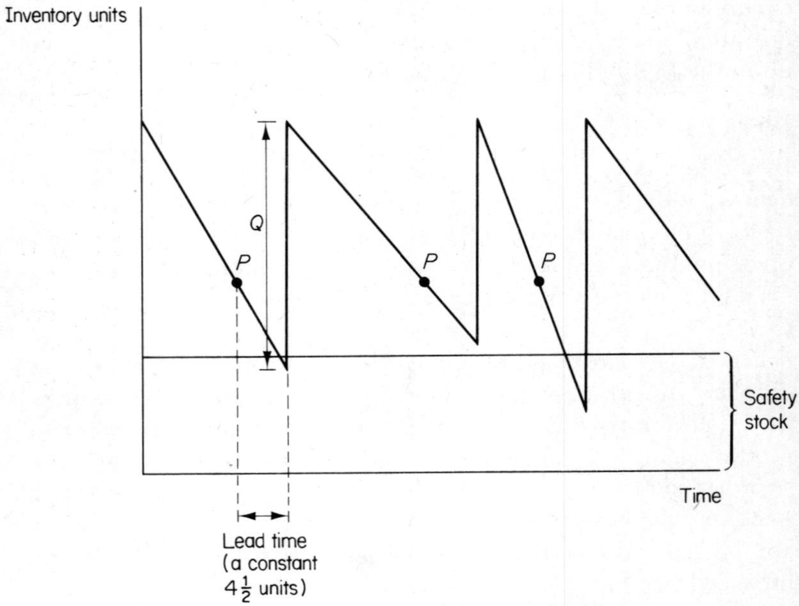

Q = Amount required to bring the stock levels up to the required level (EOQ and the safety stock)

Figure 2.8

the volatile demand can eat into the safety stocks and in such cases the order amount should be that to bring stocks up to the EOQ plus the safety stocks.

The level of safety stock will be a function of the uncertainty of demand, the uncertainty of the lead time in supplies and the costs of being out of stock. The uncertainties in demand and lead time can be reduced somewhat by measuring the variability in these items in prior years. The main measures of variability are the mean absolute deviation (MAD) and the standard deviation of the past errors of forecasting. In the case of demand functions or lead-time functions having a normal distribution, confidence limits can be applied to the forecasts and management can then specify the degree of stock-out risk it is prepared to take.

For example, Alpha forecasts daily usage at 100 units and the lead time is 20 days; the normal re-order level is therefore 2000 units. From past data, the standard deviation of demand is 5 and the standard deviation for the lead time is 1 day; the demand and lead-time variables are both normally distributed. From this, management knows that there is only a 0·135 per cent chance of daily demand being greater than 115; they also know there is only a 0·135 per cent chance of the lead time being greater than 23 days. (Tables exist which show the probability functions of normal distributions. The normal distribution tables show that there is only a 0·135 per cent chance of the forecast being more than 3 standard deviations below the actual outcome. By specifying the mean and the standard deviation the complete probabilistic distribution of a 'normal' variable can be obtained.) Thus there is a small chance (0·018 per cent, i.e. 0·135 × 0·135, if the distribution of demand and lead time are independent) of Alpha being out of stock for 5·6 days (assuming no safety stock). This is computed thus:

$$\text{Number of days stock on hand} = \frac{\text{stock}}{\text{daily demand}} = \frac{2000}{115} = 17{\cdot}4$$

Lead time = 23 days; days short of stock = 23 − 17·4 = 5·6.

Note that daily demand is at the mean plus three standard-deviation level.

Thus there is a 0·018 per cent chance of being out of stock for 5·6 days. The chances of being out of stock for other periods of time can likewise be computed. If the distributions are not normally or log-normally distributed, then the probability assumptions will not be valid. Additional considerations include:

(*a*) In the case of new products no past history will be available.

(*b*) Special occurrences may render past data irrelevant, i.e. an advertising programme may considerably alter the daily demand for finished stocks. If the demand rate is low or made up of a few orders of large quantities, then the Poisson distribution replaces the normal distribution. As with the normal, tables exist which set out probabilities of occurrence for the Poisson distribution.

(*c*) In the case of lead time, major events such as a strike may render past data irrelevant.

The costs of being out of stock must now be established. This is likely to be the current losses in profits (opportunity losses) and a subjective estimate of goodwill, i.e. the loss of profits in the longer term. The latter item is unlikely to be a linear function and therefore the total opportunity losses may look like the curve in Fig. 2.9.

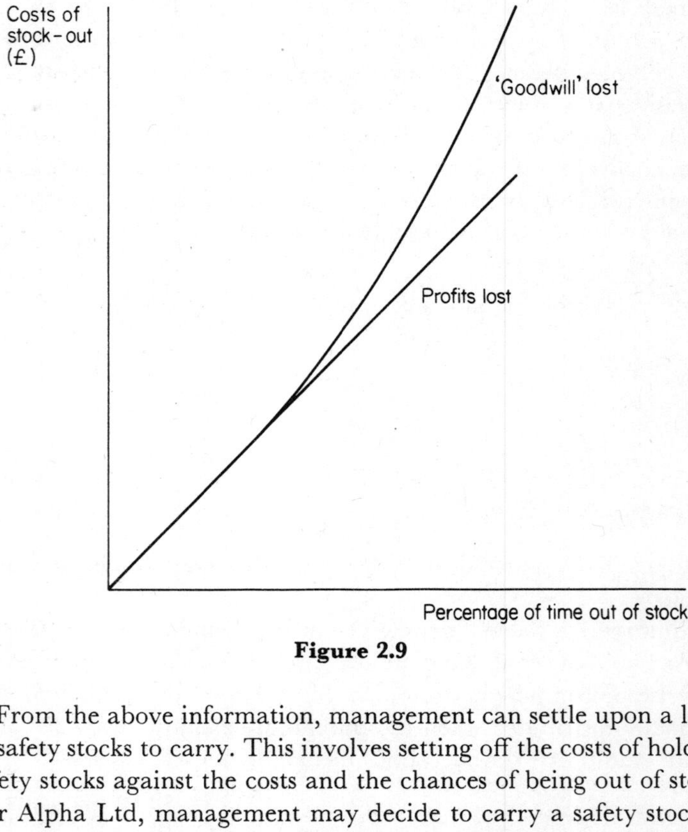

Figure 2.9

From the above information, management can settle upon a level of safety stocks to carry. This involves setting off the costs of holding safety stocks against the costs and the chances of being out of stock. For Alpha Ltd, management may decide to carry a safety stock of 690 units (this being equal to 6 days' demand at 115 units per day).

The above analyses can be employed in determining safety stocks but in a manufacturing business they will have to be carried out on the different stages of work-in-progress to calculate buffer stocks for various subassemblies or subprocesses; this will involve a good deal of data collection and arithmetic calculation. In practice, therefore, many firms rely on pure human judgement and experience in setting safety stocks.

DERIVATIVES OF THE BASIC INVENTORY MODEL

For many real-life situations the basic inventory model is an incomplete representation of the processes at work and cannot therefore give optimum results. However, sophisticated adaptations of the model have been evolved and these go a large way in meeting many of the practical problems in inventory decision-making. The main adaptations to the basic inventory model are:

(1) *Probabilistic models.* These acknowledge that the various parameters input into the inventory model are in fact random variables which may have known or unknown probability functions. In practice, both the demand functions (for example, seasonal demand) and the lead-time period are likely to have ranges of outcome and can therefore be handled by probabilistic models. The object of inventory decision-making is to minimise the total cost per period, total cost being a function of various individual sub-costs, i.e.

$$\text{Total cost} = f(Q, T, D, L, M, P),$$

where Q = quantity ordered,
T = time period of orders,
D = demand or usage rate,
L = lead time,
M = carrying costs,
P = procurement cost.

The above function is to be minimised. However, in probabilistic models the various parameters are not single-point estimates but consist of probabilistic outcomes or statistical distributions around a mean.

The probabilistic forecasts are usually handled by Monte carlo simulation techniques (discussed in Chapter 7) which produce a range of 'optimum' inventory decisions along with their associated probabilities. Probabilistic models are very costly to build and to operate; they do, however, represent a very sophisticated approach to managing inventory. An even more complex analysis is dynamic modelling where the parameters change over time; solutions may involve deriving different EOQs for different dates in the year and in order to cope with this complexity, dynamic-programming techniques have been developed. A more detailed discussion of probabilistic and dynamic models is outside the scope of the book and the interested reader should refer to the works of Brown[8] and Bellman.[9]

(2) *Quantity discounts*. Many suppliers give discounts if purchases above certain amounts are made. If the discount quantity is above the EOQ, then management will have to decide whether the value of the discount outweighs ordering a 'sub-optimum' quantity. Basically, if a discount of X per cent is available for a quantity Q greater than the EOQ, Q_0, it should only be accepted if

$$X > \frac{C_1(Q - Q_0)^2}{Q(2D - C_1)} \times 100$$

where C_1 is the inventory carrying cost as a fraction and D is the quantity per item. The analysis is continued for other quantities and discount rates.

(3) *Multi-item inventories*. In many cases companies find it impractical to differentiate certain types of stock, e.g. stocks of small hand tools. In such cases, even though the costs for these different types of stocks vary somewhat, inventory decision models have been constructed which give approximately correct solutions for groups of items.

(4) *Varying production rates and non-instantaneous production*. Where a company manufactures goods, the replenishment of finished goods is a function of the production rate. Models can be derived to handle these relationships so as to optimise the efficiency of the production and stock departments together.

(5) *Simulation of the complete stock system*. Simulation has already been mentioned in relation to probabilistic forecasting; however, it can and has been applied to complete inventory systems (order quantities, safety stocks, quantity discounts, probabilities and costs of stock-outs). If enough past data is available or if enough probabilistic forecasts can be obtained, then simulation can be carried out and this may indicate areas of weakness in the system and remedial action indicated.

(6) Models can be built which take account of other factors that have to be considered in setting optimum inventory levels. Examples include restrictions on the availability of finance and restrictions imposed by keeping to specified liquidity ratios – these may impinge on the economic order quantity. Mathematical programming models and simulation provide techniques for handling these factors.

Sensitivity of the models

The basic EOQ formula gives a single-point estimate of the optimum inventory levels. However, the various inputs can take ranges of outcome and this will produce a range of EOQs and a range of total inventory costs. One way of determining these ranges is to use probabilistic forecasting; this, however, requires considerable data and computational effort. A much cheaper method is for management to re-run the models with different inputs (possibly high, median and low estimates for each factor). It has been found that even when the inputs to the model are varied quite considerably and hence produce large changes in the EOQ, the total costs vary little. For example, Snyder[7] contends that the total-cost curves (e.g. Fig. 2.4) are rather flat over a wide range of possible EOQs. In another text, Nadder[10] has demonstrated that when all of the parameters in the simple inventory model are either under-estimated or over-estimated by 20 per cent, the effect of such errors is to increase average costs per unit of time by amounts ranging from 0·5 to 5 per cent – hardly a sensitive response. This lack of sensitivity makes the basic model quite feasible for practical use; although precise input data is expensive and difficult to obtain, the results from using approximate data will give near-optimum solutions.

Summary

Inventory accounts for a large part of many enterprises' total assets and the effective management of it is required both for the proper functioning of the normal production–selling operations of the business and for keeping the costs involved in holding stocks to a minimum. The major decisions faced by management are how much to order, when to order, what safety stocks to keep, and what stock-out probabilities and levels are acceptable. In order to assist management, various inventory decision models have been developed which help optimise solutions; these models vary in their degree of sophistication.

Once the inventories are in stock, management has to control the items. This is an extremely important function as stocks can consist of many different types, situated in various parts of the firm's premises. Detailed management-information systems are required both to give data for the decision-making and also to give data to production managers and marketing managers who will be very concerned in knowing of the stock positions in planning their own individual schedules.

The finance manager's and the accountant's roles in inventory management will almost certainly involve help in planning the management-information systems and the stock-recording procedures; it may also consist of the overall control of the inventory decision-making process. The tieing up of inventory with the other elements of working capital, cash budgeting and financing will probably also fall to the accountant and finance manager.

CHAPTER 3

The Management of Accounts Receivable

Accounts receivable or debtors represent sales that are made on credit – that is, the payments for goods are made sometime after delivery or after change in legal possession. The level of accounts receivable are a function of the level of sales, the credit terms, the riskiness of the individual customers given credit, and any seasonal influences. Although the total figure of accounts receivable may be fairly constant over time, its individual component items are continually changing and these, therefore, need careful recording and monitoring. Apart from certain retailers such as supermarkets or small 'high street' shops, most companies in fact offer credit to their customers, and by so doing the business is providing a financial service as well as the basic goods or other services. Such credit terms are desired by customers as (*a*) they may be short of ready cash at that moment in time, or (*b*) they can earn a return on the cash held during the period of credit. By making the credit terms more attractive, management can increase sales turnover; however, granting credit also involves costs of the finance tied up in accounts receivables, increased administration expenses and the probabilities of bad debts occurring. The management of accounts receivable is therefore primarily concerned with the trade-off between the profits from increased sales generated by credit policies and the costs of such policies. Other considerations that will also have to be examined include the uncertainties in the profits and costs and the impact of a receivables policy on other functions of the business, notably cash and inventory. Although competitive pressures act as a major constraint, management still has substantial scope within which to formulate accounts receivable policies. This chapter discusses the concepts behind the 'optimisation' of accounts receivable and describes analyses that can be used by management to determine credit and customer policies.

Objectives of Accounts-Receivable Management

The objective of any accounts-receivable policy should be to maximise profits. This will mean that the policy established will be that which optimises accounts receivable, inventory and cash, as a whole. For example, the liabilities structure of the company may require a certain cash balance profile to be kept. Additionally, the cost of holding stock may be so great (e.g. storage) that it may be optimum to increase the credit terms to induce advanced sales, e.g. in the cases where the cost of financing the debt is less than the storage cost of inventory. The benefits from making credit more attractive appears in the form of the increase in profits from the increased quantity sales. This will generally be:

(Sales price per unit − variable cost per unit) × the increase in the number of units sold.

If the increase in sales incurs additional fixed costs (for instance, if the factory has reached full capacity) then these must also be deducted from the sales proceeds. Before any such fixed expenses are incurred, however, management will need to form a firm opinion of the future as such fixed expenses often carry long-term obligations. As a general rule, a firm should expand credit facilities as long as the profitability of sales generated exceeds the increased cost of accounts receivable.

Responsibility of Accounts-Receivable Management

The establishment of the credit policy is largely the responsibility of the accountant. Not only is he concerned with the financing and recording of debtors and the selection of suitable customers, but he is also in the best position to assess the needs of other major activities which are connected with the level of accounts receivable, namely cash and inventory. Sales management will also be involved in formulating policies because of their knowledge of potential turnover under various credit policies and of individual customers (in order to ascertain their creditworthiness).

The main functions of accounts-receivable management are: (1) the establishment of an overall policy(ies); (2) the application of the policy to individual customers; and (3) the administration and control of the credit policy. Each of these items will be discussed in turn, below.

THE ESTABLISHMENT OF AN OVERALL POLICY

An overall policy for general credit sales has to be established because (*a*) there would be far too much work involved in establishing policies for individual customers, and (*b*) prospective customers need credit information on which to base their buying decisions. The main variables in any credit policy are: (1) the cash discount; (2) the cash-discount period; (3) the credit period; (4) the customers to accept for credit sales; and (5) the collection policy. The last two items are dealt with under the individual-customer assessment and the administration and control subheadings respectively.

A cash discount is given by the firm if a customer pays within a certain time. To the customer this represents a reduction in the price he has to pay for the goods. For example, a sale valued at £1000 is made on terms 2/10, *N*/30. This is a typical format for expressing credit terms. The first item gives the rate of discount, the second the period during which the discount is available. In this example a 2 per cent discount is given if the debt is paid within 10 days of the sale. The third term means net, and the fourth gives the maximum period for payment, in this case 30 days. Nothing has been stated about what happens if the customer does not pay within this 30 days. If the customer settles within 10 days he will only pay £980. This discount is extremely valuable to the customer as it represents an interest rate of 36 per cent per annum (by paying on day 10 instead of on day 30, a discount of 2 per cent is earned in 20 days; there are eighteen 20-day periods in a year and so the annual saving is approximately 36 per cent, i.e. 18 × 2 per cent). As we shall later see, customers who do not take advantage of this discount may be viewed with suspicion as to their solvency. Any increase in the rate of discount or any increase in the period for which it is available will lead to greater savings by the customer. This in turn will increase the quantity sales of the firm as consumers change their custom to the cheapest supplier. The increased quantity sales will not necessarily lead to an increase in profits at all stages as the financing of accounts receivable is expensive.

Apart from sales increases, the main benefit from granting discounts is that the debts are paid quicker as the discount period is less than the net date. Quicker settlements of debts gives the firm slightly more liquidity, enables them to earn more bank interest on the higher cash levels, and reduces the cost of bad debts (the longer a debt is outstanding the more chance that it may become bad, i.e.

forgetting about the account or the high cost of chasing the defaulting debtor).

In determining whether to offer a discount and, if so, at which rate and on what terms, management will need to know something about the elasticity of demand for the company's products over the feasible discount regions. This will indicate the impact on the sales quantities of the firm and from this the profitability of adopting various discount rates can be determined.

Example

At present, the company gives no discount and extends credit of 30 days; its sales are 200,000 units at a price of £1; the variable costs are equal to 60p per unit and there is spare capacity for 50,000 units. If capacity is to be raised above 250,000 units, then an immediate increase in fixed costs (new machinery and factory space) will be required, representing an annual cash outlay of £50,000. Management wants to utilise the spare capacity and considers the use of cash discounts. The sales and credit departments estimate the elasticity of demand and prepare the following summary (Table 3.1).

The example shows that by offering a discount of 5 per cent the profits of the company will be maximised; offering a higher discount of 8 per cent will lead to suboptimum results as the increased costs leads to smaller net profits. Similar analyses are required in determining the period over which the discount is given (an increase in this period will increase sales but will also incur a heavier finance charge) and in determining the net (i.e. final) payment date. An example of the latter is shown below.

Example

A company sells a product at a price of £1.00 and the cost of these sales amounts to 60p per unit. At present no credit is given at all. The firm has spare capacity for up to 50,000 units and management asks the sales and finance departments if the granting of credit would be worthwhile. These departments prepare the following summary. (Table 3.2).

The cost of financing the accounts receivable will be the opportunity cost, i.e. the return foregone by the firm in tieing up funds in debtors as opposed to investing them in the most profitable way. (Occasionally, banking sources may provide finance solely for carrying debtors; in this case, the cost of finance can be regarded as

Table 3.1

		0/0, *N*/30	2/10, *N*/30	5/10, *N*/30	8/10, *N*/30
1.	Discount rate (per cent)	0	2	5	8
2.	Unit sales	Existing 200,000	220,000	230,000	280,000
3.	Price per unit (net of discount)*	100p	98p	95p	92p
4.	Variable cost per unit	60p	60p	60p	60p
5.	Contribution margin per unit†	40p	38p	35p	32p
6.	Contribution margin (2 × 5)	£80,000	£83,600	£87,500	£89,600
7.	Increase in fixed expenses	—	—	—	£50,000
8.	Operating profits	£80,000	£83,600	£87,500	£39,600
9.	Collection expenses‡	£4000	£4000	£4000	£4000
10.	Bad-debts expenses §	£2000	£1800	£1700	£1700
11.	Net profits	£74,000	£77,800	£81,800	£33,900

* Assumes all customers take the discounts. In practice, management will estimate the percentage who do take the discount and then calculate total sales.

† Contribution margin = sales price per unit − variable cost price per unit.

‡ Collection expenses. These may rise by extending credit, i.e. administrative controls have to be set up. Against this, however, cash is collected more quickly and this can earn interest. In the example, the credit manager estimates that the impact is neutral.

§ The bad-debt expenses may fall slightly by offering discounts as it induces customers to pay more quickly – the longer a debt is left outstanding the greater the chance of it becoming bad.

the bank interest paid, assuming this does not affect the cost of capital for the remainder of the business.) The collection expenses and the bad-debts expenses are likely to increase as the length of collection period grows. The example shows that given the sales assumptions, the optimum credit period to give is 1 month.

The various exercises for establishing optimum credit periods, discount periods and discount rates can be combined to formulate an overall policy. This will require sales demand to be forecast at all the various combinations of the factors. All these analyses require knowledge of the elasticities of demand – the cost factors should be known. The elasticity functions may be appraised from trade-association figures, from the company's own statistics or the subjective judgements of the marketing department. There is almost

Table 3.2

	0 (Present Situation)	1 month	2 months
1. Credit term	0 (Present Situation)	1 month	2 months
2. Unit sales per year	200,000	230,000	240,000
3. Contribution margin per unit	40p	40p	40p
4. Contribution margin (2 × 3)	£80,000	£92,000	£96,000
5. Collection expenses	—	£500	£1500
6. Bad-debts expenses	—	£1000	£3500
7. Financing charge (10 per cent)	—	£1150	£2400
8. Net profit	£80,000	£89,350	£88,600

NOTE: The cost of finance is 10 per cent; the amounts for the two strategies, 1 month and 2 months, are calculated thus:

	1 month	2 months
1. Cost of sales (No. units × 60p)	£138,000	£144,000
2. Length of debts	1 month	2 months
3. Average investment in debtors	£11,500	£24,000
4. Interest charge (10 per cent)	£1150	£2400

certainly going to be some degree of error in these elasticity functions and, in addition, it may take time for customers to recognise the change in credit policy. Instead of specifying absolute figures, the forecasters may instead give a range of outcomes based around the 'elasticity figure' and the associated probabilities. An example of probabilistic forecasts of demand for various rates of discount is given below.

Example

The credit and the sales department specified the under-mentioned possible outcomes and their probabilities of occurrence for various rates of discount (Table 3.3).

From this data the expected values of profits can be derived for each level of discount. These figures are given in the final column of Table 3.3 and imply that adopting a 3 per cent discount rate will produce the maximum most likely profits.

Table 3.3

Rate of discount given if payment made in 10 days	Possible demand in Units						Expected value of profits (£)
	80	85	90	95	100	105	
0	0·9	0·1	—	—	—	—	2000
1	0·2	0·3	0·4	0·1	—	—	2400
2	0·1	0·3	0·4	0·2	—	—	2800
3	—	0·1	0·3	0·3	0·2	0·1	3500
4	—	—	0·2	0·4	0·3	0·1	3200
5	—	—	0·1	0·2	0·4	0·3	2700

In order to satisfy the sales demand, inventories have to be carried and in the case of uncertainty (i.e. as evidenced by the probabilistic forecasts) there may be periods of stock-outs. As holding stocks involves significant costs and as stock-outs involve lost profits, the optimising of the accounts-receivable policy needs to be conducted in conjunction with the inventory policy. An additional factor that also needs to be taken into account is the optimising of the cash position which involves assessments and date profiles of cash payments and of short-term investment opportunities.

Apart from the solutions proposed by the above analyses there are a number of other factors that may enter into credit policy-making:

(1) The need to create demand for stock that may otherwise become obsolete, e.g. fashion goods.

(2) If the customers are in a normal cyclical industrial downswing but the long-term potential appears good, then the firm may allow extended credit periods in order to help out valuable customers over short-term liquidity crises.

(3) Generous credit terms may be given as part of a promotional campaign relating to new or existing products.

(4) More generous credit terms may be given during off-season times so as to generate more consistent sales. This will allow more continuous production runs and/or reduce the level of finished inventories.

(5) Competitive pressures may force a firm to revise its policies.

This, in fact, is a major determinant in the setting of credit terms; any major deviation from the industry norms may create retaliatory pressures which often means that management has a limited scope within which to affect credit policy. Such processes can be analysed by game theory; however, this has not developed much beyond the theoretical level at present, with very few attempts having been made to implement it.

(6) Discounts are, in effect, price reductions equivalent to re-pricing the products. However, by offering the price cut in the form of a discount may reduce competitors' reactions due to their not recognising, or not recognising straight away, what has happened.

ASSESSMENT OF THE CUSTOMER FOR CREDIT

A major factor in accounts-receivable management is the accepting of new customers for credit. The aim of the credit assessment is to determine the customers who might offer significant bad-debts risks or who may be late payers of their accounts. Significant bad-debt-risk customers are not likely to be given any credit whatsoever; potential late or difficult payers may well be given small amounts of credit but on harsher terms and at higher selling prices (if it is feasible to have price differentials). The assessment of the creditworthiness of new customers is difficult but there are various standard analyses and investigations that the credit manager can make.

Investigations of the creditworthiness of a customer can be made by obtaining references and reports from various institutions (with the agreement of the debtor) and from independent agencies (without the consent of the debtor). The major sources are:

(1) *Trade references.* The customer gives the names of some of their other suppliers who will give a reference. The reliance placed upon these references depends upon the standing of the referees and of the detailed information contained in the reference. The customer has the choice of which trade suppliers he gives as references and, of course, these are likely to be favourable; the remainder could consist of dissatisfied creditors.

(2) *Bank references.* The customer's bank will give a reference on their client at their direction. This report is likely to be very general (banks have standard letters for these sort of references) and probably uninformative as banks will be reluctant to report unfavourably. It must be recognised that a customer is only likely to give trade and bank references if they are going to be favourable.

(3) *Credit agencies.* There are a number of independent credit agencies who for a fee or subscription give reports on the potential customers (two of the major companies in this field are Dunn and Bradstreet and British Debt Services). These reports are of a standard form containing financial information (usually collected from the Annual Accounts), records of poor account-keeping with other creditors and possibly a credit rating. In addition, these agencies may supply special one-off reports at the request of a subscriber.

(4) *Human judgement.* Here personal interviews, salesmen's opinions and the credit or sales manager's contacts may all contribute to the analysis of the customers' creditworthiness. If the credit manager has very extensive contacts with other firms then he may be able to glean considerable information for credit appraisal.

In using the above methods, a numerical credit-rating system can be developed. This ascribes quantitative weightings for the various factors and the granting of credit depends upon the total of these being above a certain level. Numerical credit-evaluation systems have been successfully developed for consumer credit and there is no reason why such methods cannot be successfully applied to corporate customers (see Myers and Forgy[1]).

A major method of assessing a customer's creditworthiness is to examine the financial statements of that customer – for corporate and business organisations; private customers cannot, of course, be appraised in this way. This largely involves the use of solvency and performance ratios, trends of ratios and forecasting of future profitability. Not a great deal will be covered on these assessments here as Chapter 6 covers the analysis of working capital from published accounts. The major ratios that are likely to be used include the current ratio, the quick-assets ratio, gearing structure and profit trends. Beranek[2] proposes the use of ratio model based on balance-sheet figures.

The caveats to these types of analyses covered in Chapter 6 should be borne in mind. Amongst the major considerations that have to be kept in mind are the seasonal impact of business and that major changes could have taken place since the Balance Sheet date – this being the date for which ratios can be calculated.

These analyses can be used in both determining the length of credit, if any, and the extent of credit. They are in fairly popular use and some companies, in fact, have used a number of variables jointly together in appraising creditworthiness. This has generally been effected through the use of discriminant analysis which is a multivariate statistical technique for allocating various joint variables into two or more groups. In the case of accounts receivable, the two groups would be bad or troublesome debts (i.e. very late paying) and good debts, and the analysis will involve using past data of the total accounts over a certain period. For each of the groups, various financial characteristics would be extracted such as, say, the current ratio, the quick ratio, the financial gearing and the profits growth over the past five years. Thus we would have a model of the form:

Account (designated Good or Bad) $= f$ (current ratio, quick ratio, gearing, profits growth).

The number of independent variables (those on the right-hand side of the equation) should be expanded as long as the increased accuracy of the model outweighs the costs of obtaining the data. Accuracy is measured by the better grouping of accounts such that the misclassification (e.g. accounts B and H in Table 3.4) is minimised. Discriminant analysis allows us to look at these various characteristics jointly, i.e. their overall impact. The analysis presents discriminant functions ranked in order such as that shown in Table 3.4.

Table 3.4

Customer name	State of account	Discriminant Function
A	Bad	2·41
E	Bad	2·49
C	Bad	2·54
F	Bad	2·71
L	Bad	2·89
I	Bad	2·90
B	Good	3·14
H	Bad	3·21
J	Good	3·40
D	Good	3·63
K	Good	3·81
G	Good	3·89

Management now needs to specify a cut-off point for accepting and rejecting potential credit customers. In the above example there is some misclassification, i.e. accounts B and H, but the cut-off point may well be taken at 3·15 (the midpoint of 2·90 and 3·40); or the criterion may lie in a range, e.g. reject if *f* below 2·91, accept if *f* above 3·39, and investigate further any customers with a discriminant function in the range 2·90 to 3·39.

This cut-off point or range of cut-off points will then be used to ascertain the creditworthiness of future credit applicants and to monitor existing customers. The discriminant analysis should be re-run at regular intervals to ensure that any fundamental changes in the factors influencing bad or poorly-paying accounts are recognised as early as possible. Such changes could occur in fairly short periods of time if new types are taken on, i.e. export customers, customers in new locations or the new customers for a new product.

In effecting the various analyses, management must be aware of the impact of any delay in reaching a credit decision on the patience of a customer. If a potential consumer requests an order, he will want a decision fairly quickly and so not all possible analyses will be feasible in the circumstances; therefore, it will pay, of course, to maintain an efficient credit-appraisal system. On page 59, various occasions are specified when the credit terms may be relaxed in order to stimulate sales; such occasions may also call for some relaxation on credit assessment and on the extent of credit.

For existing customers, much less detailed analysis has to be applied to their creditworthiness. As long as their payment record has been good there is little need for any investigatory work as outlined above, although a check on their annual accounts would be useful. If the customer's payments have not been kept up to date, then special care should be taken in granting further credit. Another factor that the credit manager should investigate is whether the customer takes advantage of discount opportunities. The failure to do so may indicate liquidity problems: for example, as described previously the terms 2/10, *N*/30 represent an interest rate of approximately 36 per cent – any customer who does not take advantage of this must either have very attractive investment opportunities (i.e. earning a return greater than 36 per cent) or be in a dire liquidity position. If the existing customer makes substantially larger than usual purchases, thus sending his credit requirements to much higher levels, then some reappraisment may be required by management.

The amount of credit to extend to a particular customer will depend largely upon the level of credit given previously and on how well the account has been kept. For new customers who are not especially well known or for whom little financial information exists, only small amounts of credit may at first be given. The firm may also impose certain policy limits on the amount of credit extended, for example:

(1) Individual accounts may be limited to a certain percentage of the total debtors' figure.

(2) The credit given to individual firms may be limited to a certain percentage of their net worth, net current assets or other yardstick.

If these policies are applied then it may stop over-reliance on certain customers and it may prevent giving so much credit to a customer that they become financially unstable. Many of the smaller company suppliers to Rolls Royce, for example, had over 50 per cent of their total debts tied up with them; when Rolls Royce was forced into liquidation some of the suppliers themselves became insolvent. Rolls Royce eventually paid off its debts but not until a much later date, by which time some small engineering companies had been bankrupted. If these firms had restricted their credit to Rolls Royce such that its outstanding debt represented only, say, 10 per cent of the total debts, then they may have survived. Of course, the application of such controls obviates the exercise of any human judgement on the ability of the specific customer to pay and will limit the amount of sales to perfectly creditworthy customers. In practice, therefore, the above types of limitation percentages should be used as general controls and individual assessments should be made of accounts which exceed these levels.

One method of allowing for the riskiness of individual accounts is to grant different credit terms to them. For example, a new customer or one who has had a poor payment record may be asked to pay in advance or upon delivery of the goods; additionally, the terms of credit for customers could be ranked according to their creditworthiness. In many cases, however, the latter policy may not be tenable due to both customer goodwill relations and because of administrative costs. This might also apply in attempting to charge different prices to different customers depending on their creditworthiness; for standard products it is doubtful if customers would stand for differential pricing. The major method of allowing for individual riskiness, however, is in the amount of credit extended.

The Administration and Control of Accounts Receivable

It is essential that there is an adequate management-information system in use as regards accounts receivable and that it is kept up to date (the lockbox system of paying debts, which is discussed in Chapter 4, should be considered). If not, then various overdue accounts may be neglected and the bad-debts expense and the collection of debts expense will rise sharply. Another frequently found example of the poor management of the debtors' ledger is when the customer takes the discount even though they pay after the discount date, and even after the net date! In such cases the credit manager should attempt to get the 'discount' back or refuse further credit to that customer. In addition, the control system should ensure that the credit policies laid down are adhered to. Apart from the proper recording of transactions, there are a number of summary analyses which indicate the state of the accounts receivable, the major ones being ratios of debtors to sales and the age of debtors.

The main ratio used is that which gives the accounts receivable turnover. This is

$$\frac{\text{Credit sales for the year (or other period)}}{\text{Accounts receivable}}$$

sometimes this ratio is expressed as the average age of the debt, i.e.

$$\frac{\text{Accounts receivable} \times 365 \text{ (i.e. days in a year)}}{\text{Credit sales for the year}}$$

For example, a company's credit sales amount to £12,000,000 and the total debtors are £2,000,000. The accounts-receivable turnover is, therefore, 6 (£12,000,000 ÷ 2,000,000), and the average age of the debt is 61 days, ((2,000,000 × 365) ÷ 12,000,000.)

These ratios can then be compared against those of prior periods and against budgets, and any unexpected deviations investigated. For example, the credit period may be a standard 30 days; if the actual credit period taken is much above this figure then this should act as a warning signal to the credit manager. Care has to be exercised in correctly determining the credit period to be expected;

for example, the credit terms may be 30 days net from the end of the month in which goods were bought and, if so, then a customer who buys at the beginning of the month will get as much as 60 days' credit. The ratios can be compared against those of its competitors, although the caveats of intercompany comparisons described in Chapter 6 should be heeded. Management can, of course, compile separate ratios for various classes of credit sales – this will involve separate ledger balances for, perhaps, different types of goods sold or the distinct geographical locations where sales are made.

Another major summary analysis is an age profile of the outstanding accounts. Here an analysis of the age of the debts is prepared as in Table 3.5. From this analysis, management can take

Table 3.5

Number of days the debt has been outstanding	Number of accounts	Amount (£1000)	Percentage
30	400	100	50
31–40	120	35	17·5
41–50	70	23	11·5
51–60	30	15	7·5
61–70	20	8	4
71–80	19	8	4
81–90	15	6	3
90	14	5	2·5
	Total debtors	200	100

action on accounts that have been outstanding beyond the average period of credit.

FACTORING DEBTS

Many financial companies provide factoring services for firms; this involves the financial company buying the firm's debtors for an immediate cash outlay. The type of facilities offered varies but typical examples include:

(1) Some factors agree to bear the bad debts whilst others expect to be wholly or partially reimbursed.

(2) Some factors undertake the administration of collecting debts, others do not (in which case they are unlikely to agree to bear any bad-debt expense).

These are important considerations in the control of accounts receivable – the absence of the administrative work will clearly involve substantial cost saving although the cost of the factor's services will, of course, be that much higher. The major criterion for deciding between using or not using a debt-factoring service rests on the interest costs involved since factoring is a source of short-term finance. A discussion of this choice is given in Chapter 5 on sources of finance. This chapter also briefly discusses the setting up of a subsidiary company which takes over all the debts of the operating companies within a group. Such a practice may allow a more flexible and a more profitable financing of debtors.

COLLECTION POLICY ON OVERDUE ACCOUNTS

The firm has to establish a policy as regards collecting in overdue accounts, this involving a trade-off between the expenses involved and the bad debts saved by such procedures; the default policy should be arranged in conjunction with the establishment of the credit policy. Various requests for the debt to be paid are made and these will increase in severity as the debt becomes more and more overdue; eventually legal action and debt-recovery agencies will be utilised in order to settle the debt. In planning such procedures, management must consider two main points: one is that excessive harassment of a good debtor who happens to be a few days late in one of his payments will surely loose them a valuable customer; secondly, the cost of collecting the debt and the probabilities of success need to be assessed to see if the returns will be worthwhile. Clearly, using legal action and the employment of debt-collection agencies is a costly business and they are, therefore, only used as a final resort; of course, once this final resort is required the debt will be extremely doubtful and the probabilities of recovery will be small. The relationship between expenditures on collection and the increased debts recovered is unlikely to be linear and so experience will be required in order to recognise the optimum trade-off. A simplified example of the type of data and the type of analyses required is given below.

Example

A credit manager specifies the following collection policies and their related costs:

	Policy A	Policy B	Policy C
Costs of the policy	£12,000	£25,000	£50,000
Average collection period	3 months	2 months	1 month
Percentage of debts becoming bad	3	2	1

The average collection period relates to the time between the debt occurring and it being paid; the more that is spent on collection, the faster the debts can be collected and the smaller the bad-debts expense. If the sales turnover is £1,200,000 and the cost of sales is £1,080,000 (variable costs being 90 per cent of sales proceeds), then the results of the various collection policies look like those shown in Table 3.6.

From this analysis it appears that the optimum expense to incur on collection procedures is £25,000.

In practice, more complex probabilistic models will be developed to better approximate the optimum amounts to spend on chasing doubtful debts. For an example of an actual test procedure to determine how long defaulted debts should be pursued see an article by Mitchner and Peterson[3]. The debts related to in this particular study were bank loans, although the methods could equally well relate to other type debts. There have also been a few reports[2,4] of the successful adoption of Markov chain analysis to probabilistic accounts-receivable data. However, unless and until probabilities and

Table 3.6

	A	B	C
Turnover	£1,200,000	£1,200,000	£1,200,000
Receivables Turnover*	4	6	12
Average receivables	£300,000	£200,000	£100,000
Average investment in receivables†	£270,000	£180,000	£90,000
Bad debts	£36,000	£24,000	£12,000
Cost of bad debts‡	£32,400	£21,600	£10,800

Cost of Credit Policy

1. Interest charge on average investment in receivables (10 per cent)	£27,000	£18,000	£9000
2. Bad-debts losses	£32,400	£21,600	£10,800
3. Expenses of policy	£12,000	£25,000	£50,000
Total costs of offering credit	£71,400	£64,600	£69,800

* Receivable turnover = 12 months ÷ average collection period in months.

† Average investment in receivables = Average receivables × their cost price (90 per cent of sales price).

‡ Equal to 90 per cent of bad debts.

conditional probabilities can be specified very accurately, then the practical adoption of Markov chain analysis is likely to be low.

CREDIT INSURANCE

Several insurance and financial companies offer insurance cover against bad debts. Such cover is normally only extended to specific customers or categories of customers and, additionally, the cover is usually only a percentage of the losses (say 80 per cent) from bad debts; this prevents the insured firm taking on excessively risky customers. Firms normally only take out such insurance when, say, there is an exceptionally large contract the losses from which may bankrupt the company. The most popular use of credit insurance, however, is in export sales.

EXPORT DEBTORS

The assessment of export credit requires a somewhat different approach than the assessment of home customers because (*a*) the distance factor makes it more difficult to carry out individual customer-credit assessments and (*b*) there are various risks not normally encountered with in the home market such as the changing state of diplomatic relations with foreign countries and foreign-currency movements.

As regards credit risk, the firm should make use of the knowledge of the Department of Trade and Industry and of commercial secretaries in U.K. embassies, the advice of banks who have branches or dealings with the country being dealt with, and of any credit sources within the debtor's country. The Department of Trade and Industry will give as good advice as there is on the political risks of dealing with certain countries, e.g. nationalistic governments refusing to pay for goods.

There are numerous methods of payment that can be used to settle foreign debts. Some of these require payment before or on delivery and these, of course, reduce the risk of debtor default. These methods often require the services of a U.K. or other reputable bank in the country of the debtor – any country without such representation should be dealt with cautiously. Before a firm enters export markets they must be aware of exchange-control regulations which cover the remittance of foreign currencies; this is a fairly specialised area and so advice should be sought from the DTI and from the major banks. In general, there are no real barriers to exporting but the details of the Exchange Control Act of 1947 need to be adhered to.

As with the home market, the credit manager should consider the wisdom of obtaining insurance against bad debts and, again, the decision should rest on the costs involved, the probabilities of bad debts and their impact on the business. Various financial firms offer such cover and in addition the DTI (via the Export Credit Guarantee Department, ECGD) also offers a comprehensive insurance package. The ECGD cover is particularly valid when political risks are involved – some private insurers will not provide cover for these risks. Again like the home market, the insurance will generally only cover a percentage of the debt (say 80 or 90 per cent) to help prevent the insured following an excessively liberal credit policy. The ECGD also provides financing and credit-information services to British firms exporting abroad; any firm which makes substantial exports should clearly make use of these services and those offered by the DTI.

Another risk that is usually present in export selling is the movement of foreign-exchange rates – during recent years the volatility of the major currencies against sterling has been considerable. Risk is involved when the customer is billed in his own currency (the conversion factor being that at the date of the invoice) and payment is not made until, say, two months later. By this time, sterling may have strengthened against the foreign currency and so the debt when paid realises a lesser sum than expected and budgeted for. Of course, sterling may weaken against the foreign currency in which case billing in that currency will lead to the receipt of greater amounts of pounds sterling than expected.

If management wants to reduce the uncertainty involved, it should invoice the customer in sterling and thus the exact amount to be received is known. If for some reason the customer insists on paying in their own currency, then the firm can arrange forward cover with their bankers; this involves the banker selling the foreign currency and buying sterling now at the prevailing conversion rates. When the firm receives foreign-currency payment in, say, 90 day's time, this is handed to the banker for him to cover the transaction. Most large banks will facilitate this sort of service and the costs are small.

Summary

The management of accounts receivable can be divided into three distinct areas, the establishing of a policy, the acceptance of individual credit applicants and the administration and control required. The variables under the credit manager's control include the period of the credit, the discount rate if any, and the period of the discount. The criterion for giving credit is whether it leads to greater profitability for the firm. By extending credit an increase in sales can be expected but against this the costs of the discount and of financing the debtors, the administrative costs and the bad-debts expense all have to be considered. The credit policy is set at both an overall policy level and at the individual customer level. This chapter has set out analyses and controls that can be effected in the efficient management of accounts receivable.

CHAPTER 4

Cash and Marketable Securities Management

Cash forms the method of collecting revenues and paying various costs and expenses of the business. At any one time there is almost certainly going to be a stock of cash in hand or some liability of cash owing. This is shown in the balance sheet under the headings cash in hand and bank balances or, if there is a negative bank balance, as a bank overdraft. (Note that from now on cash and current-account bank accounts will be used synonymously and deposit accounts will be treated separately with marketable securities as 'liquid assets'; the reason for the differentiation is that payments are made out of the current accounts and that it takes some time to convert deposit accounts and marketable securities into current-account cash.) The reasons for holding cash have traditionally been divided into three categories as postulated by Keynes[1], the transaction's motive, the precautionary motive and the speculative motive. Each of these will be considered in turn.

The transaction motive is the need for cash (or bank overdraft facilities) to meet the payments arising in the normal course of day-to-day business. A balance of cash is kept essentially to synchronise the receipts and payments of the business; although a company may be trading profitably the receipts from the sales are unlikely to occur, or at least unlikely to occur to the same extent, at the same time as the payments required. By holding cash balances the various day-to-day expenses can be met when due.

The precautionary motive for holding cash relates to the need for creating readily available funds to meet unexpected circumstances. the more uncertain the cash flows are, the greater the precautionary balances that have to be kept. If the company has very good access to short-term borrowing, then this acts to reduce the precautionary balances that need to be held.

The speculative motive relates to holding cash so that resources are available with which to take advantage of unusual buying opportunities. Prime examples of the use of speculative cash include investment in stocks and shares and other marketable securities, commodities, and purchasing goods (e.g. subject to a special price reduction). Apart from specialist firms such as finance and investment companies, little regular commitment is ever given to holding cash for speculative purposes. This chapter mainly relates to the transactions and precautionary motives for holding cash and unless specifically stated no further reference will be made to 'speculative motive' cash balances.

Influences Affecting the Level of Cash Balances to Hold

The major influences affecting the levels of transactions and precautionary balances held by a firm include:

(*a*) *The expected cash flows of the firm.* These will be derived from the cash budgets and forecasts prepared by the accountant. The expected cash flows will be dependent partially upon the level of sales and of the stage in the life cycle of the firm (e.g. expanding, stagnating, declining).

(*b*) *The possible deviations of cash flows.* Thus, a number of cash budgets and forecasts should be prepared, each relating to different sets of quite probable assumptions. The longer the budgeting and forecasting period the greater these deviations will be; however, longer-term uncertainties do not impose severe problems for the current liquidity position.

(*c*) *Major non-recurring expenditures such as the building of a new factory or the purchase of a ship.* If such expenditures are forecast well in advance (usually they are planned expenditures and so management has time to formulate financing arrangements) and they are very large in relation to the remainder of the business activities, then management may have to build up liquid resources over some period of time. These will be invested in revenue-earning liquid assets (deposit accounts or marketable securities) pending the expenditure.

(*d*) *The repayment (maturity) structure of the firm's outstanding debt.* If such debt cannot be repaid out of the proceeds of a new issue of long-term debt (because, say, of poor capital-market conditions), then management will have to liquidate various assets. As in (*c*) above, this is likely to be done over a longish period.

(*e*) *The firm's borrowing capacity to meet emergency needs.* If these are good, then less transaction and precautionary balances are required. This borrowing capacity is likely to be governed by three major factors: (1) the firm's relationship with its bankers and its general creditworthiness appearance; (2) the presence of any security that can be offered against the short-term borrowing, i.e. marketable securities and unencumbered property assets; and (3) the general state of the money markets and of the prevailing bank-borrowing conditions.

(*f*) *Management's attitude to running out of cash.*

(*g*) *The efficiency of the control of cash.*

The balances held in cash depend upon management's policies (explicit or implicit) as regards cash and working capital, the level of sales, accounts receivable and inventory. Without any change in policies one would expect the cash balances to move largely in line with the level of sales. For seasonal businesses, cash balances may vary with the time of year; for example, greetings-card manufacturers may expect very heavy cash inflows just before Christmas as retail shops purchase Christmas cards. In the case of seasonal businesses and especially those without continuous production, the optimisation models presented later on may not be very viable, or at least not very viable without a good deal of adjustment; the management of cash in these businesses may therefore require much more subjective judgement. Apart from any possible seasonal bias, management has complete control of cash and so its efficient usage is in its hands.

Objectives in Managing Cash

The main objective in managing cash is to trade-off liquidity and profitability in order to maximise long-run profits. By keeping greater amounts of current-account cash (liquidity), the firm is more able to meet its debts (both expected and unexpected) and thus creditor confidence is kept and the risk of technical insolvency reduced. However, current-account cash does not earn any interest and so the greater amounts of resources left as cash balances, the less the profits-earning potential of the firm; in extreme cases this lack of profitability will result in shareholder dissatisfaction and takeovers. If cash balances were reduced to nil, then the very short-term profitability of the firm should rise as the resources are invested in revenue-earning assets; in the longer term, however, the damage to credit impairment caused by shortage of liquidity will almost certainly lead to reduced profits (e.g. difficulties in obtaining supplies at competitive prices and at the right time). Management, therefore, has to formulate policies about the level of liquidity to keep at any moment in time.

Apart from liquidity in the form of cash balances, management can also invest resources in 'near-money' assets. These primarily involve deposit accounts with both banks and the money market, and marketable securities in the form of Stock Exchange quoted fixed-interest stocks and quoted equity shares. The advantages of these assets is that they can earn a return and yet they can easily be converted into cash. There is some delay, and for some assets uncertainty, in the conversion of 'near-money' assets and so some balance of current-account cash is required. Generally speaking, the more liquid the asset, the lower the return on it will be; marketable securities in normal times do not earn as high returns as investment in plant and machinery, inventories and debtors (if the returns are as great for a particular company, then this implies that it should turn itself into an investment trust and hold securities solely). Liquidity is generally measured by (1) the speed of conversion into cash, i.e. 1 day, 7 days, 14 days, and (2) whether there is any uncertainty in the cash amounts realised from the sale of the security (i.e. stocks and shares values can vary). The characteristics of a marketable-securities portfolio are dealt with later in the chapter. So in deciding the levels of liquidity to be maintained, management needs to determine the division between cash and marketable securities and deposits; this generally means keeping as little cash as possible and investing as much as possible in trading assets.

The management of cash is usually vested in the accounting and finance executives of the company because of their knowledge of short-term borrowings, short-term investment opportunities and their responsibilities in preparing budgets. In large organisations there are often separately designated 'Treasury' departments where several personnel are concerned with cash management. For the more sophisticated cash-decision models, some operational research and statistical skill may be required.

Costs of Being Short of Cash

The 'costs' of being short of cash come in the form of not being able to take advantage of discounts and short-lasting special buying opportunities, and that of credit impairment. Discounts for paying cash promptly are usually very generous and the effective return on capital employed is often well above that earned on any other asset. To take advantage of a discount, cash is required to be paid in very short periods of time; often there is insufficient time for funds from marketable securities and deposit accounts to be transferred to cash (e.g. bank deposit transfers usually require seven days' notice – this is too long if a company wishes to take advantage of a discount which lasts for a period of five days). The impact of not being able to take advantage of a cash discount is therefore quite significant.

The impact of liquidity shortage as regards creditworthiness is difficult to quantify but it can be very serious. The ramifications of credit impairment can mean:

(1) No credit given – all dealings for cash. Alternatively, the credit terms could be made less generous.

(2) Creditors could mark their prices up in order to compensate for poor payments.

(3) Suppliers may refuse to deal at all.

(4) Suppliers may give slow or unreliable delivery times. If there is an excess of demand for supplies, then the poor-paying firm may find that it is the last on the list of priority customers.

(5) Short-term and long-term financing will not be so easily obtainable or on such generous terms.

(6) In some cases the shortage of cash may lead creditors to petition for a winding up of the firm. This has very adverse publicity effects. In some cases if the company has invested in difficult-to-realise assets, it may be forced into liquidation. There have been numerous cases where companies with sound and profitable assets have been forced into bankruptcy through lack of cash – it being impossible to sell the assets quickly and at a realistic price.

The quantification of credit impairment is difficult and will probably have to be subjectively estimated. Apart from the loss of creditor confidence, a strained liquidity position also places pressures on individual managers. The amount of time spent by senior executives to satisfy creditors when the cash balances are low is likely to be very costly.

Methods for Establishing Cash Balance Levels

In helping management determine the trade-off between liquidity and profitability, there are a number of analyses and model-building approaches that can be utilised which help forecast cash flows in future periods and determine the amounts of cash and marketable securities to hold and when to effect transfers between these.

CASH BUDGETS

One of the main methods of planning and controlling the investment in cash is to prepare detailed cash budgets; these are period-by-period forecasts of future cash flows of the business. From the budgets, management has an estimate of when additional finance will be required and when surplus funds are likely to arise. This gives notice to the firm so that, say, short-term financing can be arranged in plenty of time in the case of cash shortages and that short-term investment opportunities can be investigated in the case of surplus funds. Alternatively, the budget may be used for planning purposes and, upon seeing the likely cash flows resulting from the extrapolation of current policies, management may decide to, say, alter its accounts-receivable and inventory policies in order to utilise or free cash resources; the implementation of alternative policies will create new cash-flow profits and so revised budgets will be required. The detailed make-up of cash budgets will be needed in building cash models which are described later.

Cash budgets can be made over various time horizons; these horizons are divided into periods for which cash balances are calculated. For the purposes of working-capital management, it is the short-term horizon, say one year, which is important – although regard should still be had for longer-term cash-flow estimates. The periods for which the cash flows are computed depends upon the nature of the business but generally they should be at least monthly. If the cash inflows and outflows fluctuate greatly then a weekly forecasting period will be required. In many companies a weekly budget is prepared for the immediate future, say three months, then a monthly budget up to say twenty-four months hence with a quarterly forecast thereafter. The adoption of such a procedure is for two main reasons: firstly, more detailed forecasts are needed in the short term and, secondly, the short term can be more accurately forecast and so weekly budgets become tenable. The construction of a cash budget is described below.

A monthly cash budget for Alpha Ltd over a six-month time horizon is shown below. The normal cash receipts of the firm are in respect of sales. Therefore, sales forecasts for the forthcoming

Table 4.1

	Nov.	Dec.	Jan.	Feb.	March	April	May	June	July
					£000				
Cash sales	—	—	11	11	11	15	16	14	12
Credit sales	48	50	52	50	54	58	60	60	58
Receipts:									
Cash sales	—	—	11·0	11·0	11·0	15·0	16·0	14·0	—
Credit sales									
First month 10%	—	—	5·2	5·0	5·4	5·8	6·0	6·0	—
Second month 80%	—	—	40·0	41·6	40·0	43·2	46·4	48·0	—
Third month 10%	—	—	4·8	5·0	5·2	5·0	5·4	5·8	—
Total receipts			61·0	62·6	61·6	69·0	73·8	73·8	—
Purchases (60% of next month's sales	—	37·8	36·6	39·0	43·8	45·6	44·4	42·0	—
Payments									
Purchases (paid one month after purchase)	—	—	37·8	36·6	39·0	43·8	45·6	44·4	—
Wages	—	—	5	5	5	6	6	6	—
Administrative expenses	—	—	4	5	4	5	6	5	—
Selling expenses	—	—	3	4	4	5	4	5	—
Capital expenditure	—	—	—	—	—	30	—	—	—
Other expenses	—	—	6	12	11	7	6	10	—
Total payments			55·8	62·6	63·0	96·8	67·6	70·4	—

Net cash flow and cash balance (£000)

	Jan.	Feb.	March	April	May	June
Cash receipts	61	62·6	61·6	69·0	73·8	73·8
Cash payments	55·8	62·6	63·0	96·8	67·6	70·4
Net cash flow	5·2	—	(1·4)	(27·8)	6·2	3·4
Opening cash balance	20·0	25·2	25·2	23·8	(4·0)	2·2
Closing cash balance	25·2	25·2	23·8	(4·0)	2·2	5·6

six-month period are required and these are shown on the top two lines of Table 4.1; these will usually be obtained from the marketing department. If the firm is selling established products and there have been no recent unusual factors (i.e. promotional campaigns, no new products from competitors, no sudden economic slump), then the sales forecasts will probably be fairly accurate. Chapter 7 covers forecasting techniques applicable to business and economic data. The sales forecasts are probably the most important in budgeting as forecasts and planning of other activities are based on the sales estimates.

The next step for the accountant is to derive cash flows from the sales estimates. This will depend upon the credit terms of the firm and historical experience of customers' attitudes to payment (i.e. whether they take discounts or not, whether they pay by the stated net date). If the products are well established and if the credit terms applicable to the various product lines are similar, then fairly accurate estimates of cash inflows can be made. In the case of Alpha Ltd, 10 per cent of credit sales in any month are received in cash during that month, 80 per cent in the next month and 10 per cent in the third month. From this the total cash receipts are computed; if there are any other receipts (rental income, dividend income, capital monies, proceeds from sale of assets), then these should be added in.

The level of the normal day-to-day operating expenses are a function of sales (in some cases this may not be true, i.e. where inventories are being run down or increased, e.g. fireworks manufacturers where production is continuous but sales only made in one or two months). The various raw-material costs and production expenses can be obtained from the production schedules; other regular expenses should be easily calculated given a sales figure. In preparing the cash budget some expenses may be paid later than the month they were incurred; in Alpha's case the purchases were paid for one month after their acquisition. The accountant will know the various credit terms given by suppliers and should be able to compute the dates of cash payment for various goods and services received; any non-regular expenditure should also go into the cash budget; common examples include taxes, dividends, debt repayments and capital expenditures. The dates and amounts of payments relating to these items will generally be known well in advance so there will be no uncertainty in the forecasting. In the example, Alpha spends £30,000 on capital expenditure in April.

From the forecast cash receipts and cash payments the net cash flow can be calculated (the difference between the two figures). This is then added or subtracted from the opening balance to obtain the closing cash balance at the end of the month.

From the cash budget, management can see that they need some short-term finance in April to meet the forecast negative balance. The policies open to them include:

(1) the sale of marketable securities during April to cover the negative balance;

(2) if there are no marketable securities then liquidation of other assets can be undertaken;

(3) short-term borrowing from banking sources;

(4) a planned programme of paying some creditors later than usual.

By forecasting the situation several months in advance, management has time to consider various alternatives and is not hurried into ill-considered decisions. Once management has decided upon its policy as regards the negative cash balance at the end of April, the cash budget should be redone to show the impact of this. The cash budget can also reveal high cash balances and, depending on how long these are expected to be maintained, various investment opportunities can be considered. Generally, long-term deposits earn higher rates of interest; if the surplus cash position is only expected to last for two months say, then the long-term deposit investment is unsuitable.

Apart from the mean estimate prepared above, management will want to have some idea of the variability of the cash flows; the budgets should therefore be re-run using different possible outcomes. In practice, this may amount to around five different forecasts including a high and a low estimate. The assumptions relating to the different forecasts should be explicitly stated and set out in the budget report. If probabilities can be attached to these estimates this will considerably assist management in appraising the budget and in determining policies.

SOURCES AND USES OF FUNDS STATEMENTS

Some authors advocate the use of sources and uses of funds statements to aid working-capital management and cash control. However, these do not give as much information as the cash-budgeting process just discussed; indeed, the statements require cash budgets in order for them to be computed. Sources and uses statements are of more use to outside parties who are appraising a firm for credit, lending or investing purposes. An analysis of these statements is given in Chapter 6.

Decision Models for Cash Management

The cash budget gives forecasts of future cash flows and from this management has to make various decisions regarding the levels of cash balances to carry and when to transfer monies to a marketable-securities account (from now on this term will incorporate deposit accounts). These decisions have traditionally been subjectively based but recent research has shown that objective decision models can be successfully applied and, subject to the accuracy of the data input, they give optimal solutions. Specifically, the models give deterministic solutions to:

(1) the minimum and maximum levels of cash balances;
(2) the minimum and maximum amounts of marketable securities to hold;
(3) the dates for transferring funds between marketable securities and cash;
(4) the costs of being out of cash and the trade-off policy with the expenses of holding cash.

These models can also give probabilistic results and by simulating the complete system of cash, accounts receivable and inventories, an overall optimal solution can be derived. The models require fair amounts of data to establish the weightings and parameters and some of this information may be difficult to obtain or may require subjective estimates. In companies with very erratic cash flows (perhaps a young, fast growing firm) these models may have to be reappraised at frequent intervals to ensure they still fit the circumstances.

INVENTORY DECISION MODELS FOR CASH MANAGEMENT

Cash can be considered as an inventory held to meet future demands and thus the well-known inventory decision models, as described in Chapter 2, can be applied. Thus, given data on the demand for cash, the transactions costs of obtaining cash (i.e. brokerage costs) and the holding costs (principally interest paid or the opportunity costs of interest foregone), the model can determine the amount of cash to be held and when transfers should be made from marketable securities to cash, and from other non-liquid assets into marketable securities.

Thus let:

QM = the optimum amount of cash to be obtained from other sources at optimum time intervals,

DM = the amount of cash that is expected to be used in the next time period; this is the payments less receipts,

FC = fixed costs of transactions expenses incurred in obtaining cash, and

HC = holding cost of money.

The optimum amount of cash to raise is given by the square-root inventory formula:

$$QM = \sqrt{\frac{2\ (FC)\ (DM)}{HC}}$$

(See Chapter 2 for the derivation of this formula. Its application to cash is exactly the same; $QM = Q$, $FC = F$, $DM = D$, $HC = C$, in the inventory model of Chapter 2.)

Thus, if $DM = £50{,}000$, i.e. the cash payments are £50,000 greater than cash receipts in the period (say one month); $FC = £50$, this represents a fixed cost per transaction; $HC = 10$ per cent, then the optimum quantity of cash to raise on each occasion is:

$$QM = \sqrt{\frac{2 \times 50 \times 50{,}000}{0{\cdot}10}}$$

$$= £7071$$

The total cost (TC) involved in holding cash balances will be thus:

$$TC = \frac{DM \times FC}{QM} + DM \times VC + \frac{HC \times QM}{2}$$

where VC is the variable transaction cost, if any (e.g. brokerage cost on the sale of securities). If the variable costs in the example is, say 1 per cent, then the total cost of holding cash becomes

$$TC = \frac{50{,}000 \times 50}{7071} + 50{,}000 \times 0{\cdot}01 + \frac{0{\cdot}10 \times 7071}{2}$$
$$= 353{\cdot}5 + 500 + 353{\cdot}5$$
$$= £1207$$

The inventory model is also used to determine the optimum amount of cash and marketable securities to purchase (see Baumol[2]). This model then goes on to determine the amount of the transfer between marketable securities and cash for various subperiods. Additionally, the various modifications to the basic inventory model as described in Chapter 2 can also be applied to cash. In practice, however, the basic inventory model is the most than companies have attempted.

Whilst the inventory approach describes the nature of cash flows, the basic model itself incorporates assumptions which, especially in the case of corporate enterprises, are not valid. (The basic inventory-model approach is much more appropriate to individuals, i.e. they withdraw money from a bank deposit account once a week or once a

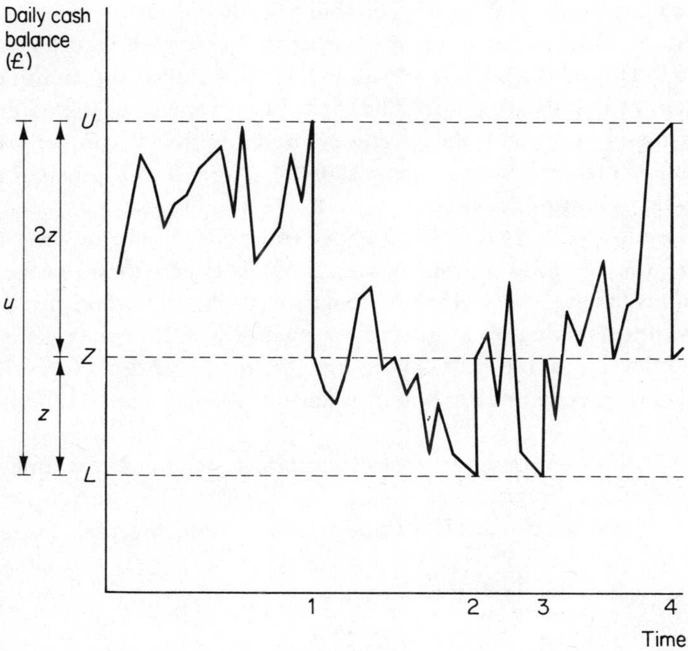

Figure 4.1

month to meet their daily expenses.) Principally, the model assumes a constant demand for cash overtime but this is unlikely to be an accurate representation of a firm's cash flows which are likely to be of a pattern similar to Fig. 4.1, where on some days receipts are greater than payments and where the net difference between receipts and payments varies between different days. If receipts exceed payments for a certain period of time and the cash balance reaches a high level, then management may purchase securities in order to earn a return on surplus cash. Thus, in most cases, the basic inventory model only gives a very crude approximation of the cash-flow situation of a firm.

THE MILLER–ORR MODEL[3,4]

Miller and Orr have developed a model which expands upon the basic cash inventory model by assuming that the net cash flows are random in direction (positive or negative) and that they form a normal distribution as the number of observations increase. Their model allows for *a priori* knowledge that at certain times the net cash flows have a greater probability of being either positive or negative. Thus the model can incorporate the known fact that, say, payments exceed receipts on Fridays (pay days) or at the month end (when trade bills are paid). The main improvement of the Miller – Orr model over the basic inventory model is that it can represent cash flow processes such as those shown in Fig. 4.1 – in other words, real-life cash-flow processes.

The model allows the cash balance to wander freely between two levels and, as long as the balance stays between these levels, no action is taken. If and when the balance reaches the upper limit U, a transfer is made into marketable securities such that the cash level falls to level Z; if the cash balance reaches the lower limit L, a sale of marketable securities is made in order to replenish cash to the level Z.

The Miller – Orr model seeks to minimise the total cost function for a given minimum level of cash (the level L). The decision rules given by the model are the upper level, U, and the cash re-order level Z (equal to $Z^* + L$) (asterisks* represent optimum values). The cost function is stated thus:

$$E(c) = \frac{aE(N)}{T} + iE(M)$$

where $E(c)$ = expected cost,

a = cost per transfer between cash and securities,

$E(N)$ = expected number of transfers between cash and securities,

T = number of days in the planning period,

i = daily rate of return on the securities,

$E(M)$ = expected average daily cash balance.

For the special case where p (the probability that cash balances will increase) = 0·5 and q (the probability that the cash balances will decrease) = 0·5, the solution proposed by the model becomes

$$Z^* = \frac{(3a\sigma^2)^{1/3}}{(4i)}$$

and $U^* = 3Z^*$ (in this special case the upper control limit (U) is always 3 times greater than the amount Z; this is the situation shown in Fig. 4.1),

σ^2 = the variance of the daily changes in cash balances.

The solution gives the following decision rules:

(1) When the cash balance rises to U^*, buy securities amounting to £$2Z^*$. This reduces the cash balance to £Z^* + the minimum level (L). See time points 1 and 4 in Fig. 4.1.

(2) When the cash balance falls to the level L, sell securities amounting to £Z^*. This increases the cash balance to $Z^* + L$. See time points 2 and 3 in Fig. 4.1.

Probabilities other than those of the case $p = q = 0{\cdot}5$ (this being quite a common case, however), can be incorporated in the cost function to obtain values for U^* and Z^*.

To use the model, a fair amount of accurate data is required and this may be difficult to acquire and may often hinge on subjective estimates. For example, estimates are required of the expected number of transfers between cash and securities (i.e. how often net cash flows are likely to be at the upper or lower limits) and what the expected average cash balances are going to be. The cost of transfers includes the time of management in dealing with the transfers and this usually requires some subjective judgement. In addition, the model requires that management specify a minimum cash level (L);

this level will almost certainly be subjectively appraised; amongst the factors that management will consider are:

(1) the level of uncertainty;
(2) the extent of fluctuations in cash balances; and
(3) the 'costs' of being out of cash.

The next section gives one analysis that may help management to determine the minimum cash level. Despite the above, Miller and Orr found that the model produced considerable costs savings when applied to a large industrial company; later investigations have similarly found the model to effect significant savings.

There are two major conceptual assumptions in the model, however, which need to be considered. One is that the variance is used as the measure of dispersion in the cash flows. Whilst this is tenable in a relatively predictable and stable situation, the model may well give suboptimal results if the net cash flows change by very large amounts in short periods of time. The second assumption is that shortages in cash (i.e. at point *L*) are met from transfers of marketable securities. In many cases, however, management may be in a position to borrow and this alternative may be cheaper than selling securities (indeed the firm may have to borrow if cash is required immediately – before the proceeds of the sale of marketable securities can be received). The Miller–Orr model does not consider this alternative, however. The potential of borrowing to meet shortages of cash, therefore, has to be handled subjectively as an additional factor; a number of other models do incorporate borrowing decisions into their solutions and one will be discussed next.

BERANEK'S MODEL

Beranek[5] has postulated a probabilistic model for controlling cash which involves management specifying probabilistic outcomes for net cash flows (this based on prior knowledge and experience). The model also requires figures for the costs of being short of cash for various periods. The main costs identified by Beranek were:

(1) the loss of cash discounts; and
(2) the impairment of credit.

The latter in particular will require subjective judgement and the impact is unlikely to be linear (the ramifications of the impairment of credit were mentioned on page 75). Apart from these, management may be able to specify other costs of being out of cash.

Beranek's model determines the allocation of funds between cash and marketable securities at the beginning of the period with transfers only taking place at the end of the period. The model assumes that receipts of cash are continuously taking place and that they fluctuate in value; payments, on the other hand, are assumed to take place on certain days (or at least not continuously). The cash-flow procedure would therefore look something like that in Fig. 4.2; note

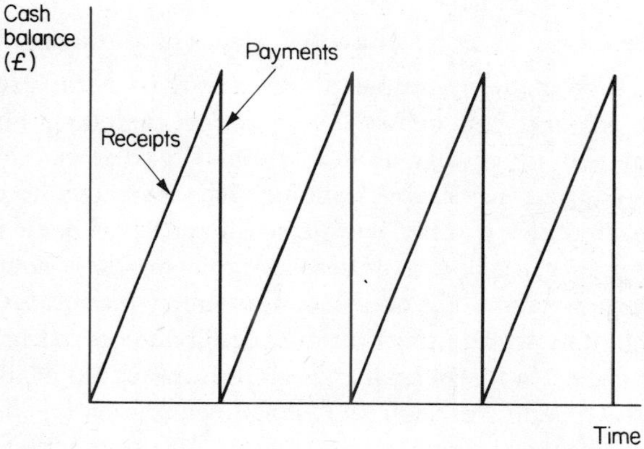

Figure 4.2

that this contrasts with the basic inventory model described earlier where demand for cash was considered a continuous variable and receipts taking place at one particular time (i.e. $(DM/QM) \times$ time period). The rationale behind Beranek's cash-flow process is that firms often arrange to pay their bills at the end of the month (wages may be paid on the Friday of each week or at the month end) whilst receipts are continuous (e.g. proceeds from cash sales).

The inputs to Beranek's model are the probabilistic estimates of cash flows, transaction costs, the costs of running short of cash and the opportunity costs of holding cash. The costs of running short of cash can perhaps be best estimated by the interest that is paid on the borrowings that cover the shortage (assuming that such borrowings are available); Beranek, however, actually applied the costs of running out of cash but this involves highly subjective estimates and makes the model difficult to apply. The cost of borrowing could also be applied to the discount foregone, as by borrowing the firm can take advantage of the discount; it may be, however, that borrowings cannot be arranged at such short notice. The model develops a cost function and this is differentiated to give the optimum cash balance that should be on hand at the start of each period. This minimum level is such that the expectation of the closing cash balance being below this level is equal to the ratio of the marginal net return per £ of investment in securities to the marginal cost of being short of cash per £.

A COMPARISON OF THE MILLER–ORR AND BERANEK MODELS

The Miller–Orr model is simpler to operate than Beranek's probabilistic model and can be used over longer planning horizons. Beranek's model and its various adaptations (e.g. that of White and Norman[6]) require considerable data and its parameters need to be reassessed each time a transfer between cash and securities is made – this does, however, make it more sensitive to changes in conditions. Model approaches should be used in conjunction with management's own judgement in determining optimum cash balances to keep; they should be applied to the normal every-day transactions of the firm. Exceptional expenditures such as tax payments, major capital expenditures and long-term debt repayments will have to be handled outside of the model – as these expenditures are known some time in advance no great problems should arise in their planning.

DETERMINING THE MINIMUM CASH BALANCE

One analysis that management can conduct in determining a minimum cash balance to carry is to construct a probability distribution of a firm's day-to-day change in net cash flows. This analysis should ignore major items which are known with certainty as these can be planned for separately. The distribution is prepared from recent historical data and it may look like Fig. 4.3. The area under the curve represents the probabilities and management can now specify what chance it is willing to take of being short of cash. If, for example, management was prepared to accept a 5 per cent chance of having no cash during a day, then the cash balance to maintain is £50,000, i.e. in only 5 per cent of cases will the daily net cash flow be greater than minus £50,000. If management was more conservative and decided a 1 per cent cash-out probability was all

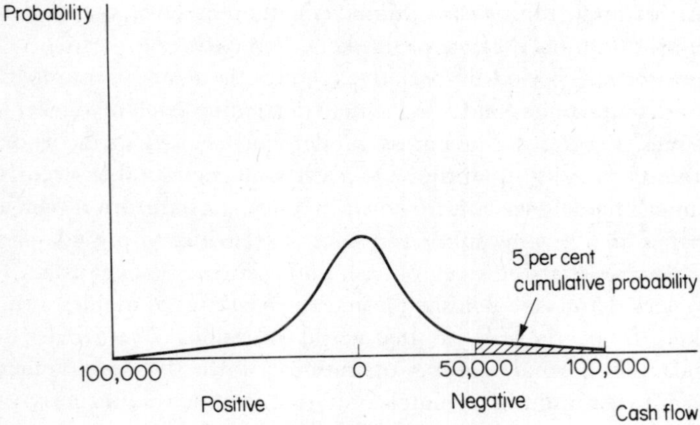

Figure 4.3

that it could accept, then the minimum cash balance would have to be raised to approximately £95,000. This type of analysis is tenable where the net cash-flow changes are not too erratic; if the distribution is approximately represented by a normal distribution, this will aid the assessment of probabilities. Management's preference as regards being out of cash will be a subjective appraisal of their cash-out aversion, and to the costs of being short of cash and to the availability of immediate short-term borrowing. (It is possible of course to have successive days showing negative net cash flows; however, it is assumed that the cash balances can be replenished from a sale of marketable securities at one day's notice; the optimum balance for marketable securities is dealt with later.)

DETERMINING THE BALANCE OF MARKETABLE SECURITIES TO HOLD

The analyses have so far determined the optimum cash balances to hold and that these are replenished from marketable securities and deposit accounts (borrowing is another possibility but this depends largely upon uncertain relations with bankers). Thus a stock of liquid assets are held to augment the cash balance or to mop up temporary surplus cash. These marketable securities, however, are not expected to earn as high a return as investments in fixed assets, inventories or debtors and, therefore, any 'surplus' of these securities incurs an opportunity cost. Management, therefore, has to determine an optimum balance of marketable securities to keep.

For normal period-by-period expenses there are a number of analyses that can be conducted to help determine levels of marketable securities. Firstly, the inventory model can be used to incorporate optimum re-order quantities of cash and marketable securities (Baumol's model[2] sets out to show the re-order quantities of cash and securities and to show subperiod sales of securities to provide cash). This assumes that the stock of cash and securities is exhausted over some period and is replenished from, say, new capital monies – this is unlikely to be the case in real-world situations where over long periods the normal trading operations of the business generate sufficient cash inflows to match outflows. Profits account for by far the largest source of annual finance raised by British companies.

Perhaps a more appropriate analysis is that suggested by Stancill[7] which involves calculating the probabilities of successive negative net cash flows, best described by the use of an example. From the probability distribution shown in Fig. 4.3, we see that the 'maximum' negative daily net cash flow is £100,000. Thus, at least £100,000 must be held in marketable securities, i.e. this replenishes the cash balance to its desired minimum level. However, it is possible that the next day will also show a maximum negative cash flow and this will have to be met from marketable securities. The chances of a decrease in the second day is 0·50 and so the amount provided for is £100,000 × 0·5. (If the probability of an increase–decrease is not 50–50, then the appropriate factor will have to be applied. Such other probabilities are likely if the firm is expanding or declining rapidly.) The probability of there being a negative net cash flow for three successive days is $1 \times 0{\cdot}5 \times 0{\cdot}5 = 0{\cdot}25$ and the maximum deficit of £100,000 multiplied by 0·25 gives the probability outcome of £25,000. Table 4.2 lists the various probable outcomes; the total of these tends towards a value of £200,000 and this represents the optimal balance to keep in marketable securities. The balance represents the probability of there being successive negative net cash flows multiplied by the greatest possible value of a negative cash flow.

There are other probability models that could be derived to obtain optimum securities levels. In the Stancill model, the maximum possible negative net cash flow was multiplied by the probability of there being a cash decrease. However, the cash decrease could take the range £1 to £100,000 and in fact the chances of a loss of

Table 4.2

Day	Probability of successive decreases	Summation of probability of successive decreases times maximum negative cash flow (£100,000) (£)
0	1·00	100,000
1	0·5	50,000
2	$0{\cdot}5^2$	25,000
3	$0{\cdot}5^3$	12,500
4	$0{\cdot}5^4$	6,250
5	$0{\cdot}5^5$	3,125
.	.	.
.	.	.
.	.	.
16	$0{\cdot}5^{16}$	1
		£199,611

£100,000 occurring are less than 1 in 100. Other criteria could include multiplying the probability of successive cash decreases by the expected value of the negative cash deficit. Additionally, more complex conditional probability models can be built to explain the process. If a large negative cash flow occurs it may be because a major customer has not paid his bill on the day expected and this may imply that a large positive cash flow will occur the next day when the bill is paid. The treasurer or accountant should investigate the probability distribution of past net cash-flow changes and then derive a suitable model; this may involve simulation of the system to obtain an accurate representation.

Apart from the model approach based on the net cash flows, the marketable-securities balance should also include resources being saved up to meet large expenses. For example, many firms have to pay their tax bills on 1 January in each year. The funds to pay for this expense will be invested in various short-term assets (including inventories and receivables); as 1 January approaches the funds will be transferred into very liquid assets, i.e. marketable securities, pending the transfer to cash to meet the tax bill. Many large, known expenditures can be planned for several months in advance and the funds for these should be invested in marketable securities as the payment date nears (investing in inventories and receivables will add to the uncertainty as their realisation into cash may take several weeks).

Another consideration that affects the marketable-securities balance is the firm's banking relationships; if these are good then it means that the securities balance can be reduced. Generally, very short notice bank borrowing is expensive but if the probabilities of the daily net cash flows being negative are small and the firm's other investment opportunities are very good, then it may pay to keep the liquid-assets balances low.

CONTROL OF CASH AND BANKING FACILITIES

Management can use various ratios to examine the use of cash in the business activities; one often-quoted is that of cash turnover or cash velocity and is computed thus:

$$\text{cash turnover} = \frac{\text{sales per period}}{\text{initial cash balance}}$$

The higher the turnover, the less the cash balance required for any given level of sales and, other things being equal, implies greater efficiency. This ratio can be used to establish the cash balance to be held; once the sales forecasts for various periods have been made the required cash balance can be calculated using historical cash-turnover figures. (If the cash-balance analyses referred to earlier cannot be undertaken for some reason, then the cash turnover provides some yardstick for setting cash balances.) The ratios should be computed at various times in the year, especially if the business is seasonal, and can be compared against prior-year statistics; any unexpected deviations should be investigated.

The firm should take as much action as it can to speed up the collection of cash and it should ensure that their bankers process deposits as quickly as possible. Slack control in these areas can lose substantial interest; if all the proceeds from sales can be deposited in interest-earning assets, say two days earlier than usual, substantial interest could be earned. For example, if sales proceeds were £10,000,000 and by tight control they can be deposited two days earlier, then extra interest of £5479 ($10{,}000{,}000 \times 0{\cdot}10 \times (2/365)$) could be earned (the interest rate at 10 per cent).

The speeding up of debtor payments is, of course, largely the responsibility of the accounts-receivable policies. However, there is often considerable scope for tightening up the delivery of cash – this is the time it takes from the payment leaving the debtor to it being banked by the firm. Amongst the procedures that can be adopted by the firm are:

(1) To obtain a direct debiting agreement with the client. By this method the firm instructs the customer's bank when they should pay. This prevents the customer from delaying payment by oversight or for any other reason and, additionally, the transfer to the firm's bank can be made on the same day. However, only customers receiving a very regular service (e.g. a monthly payment on a contract for supplying, say, a regular delivery of chemicals to a pharmaceutical company) are likely to agree to direct-debit transactions.

(2) To request the bank to make an express clearance of cheques. Many cheques take two or three days to clear and it is only then that interest can be earned on a deposit account or payments made against the receipt. The request to the bank to clear cheques quickly should be directed principally to the very large receipts – if the firm has good relationships with its bank and if they, say, deposit short-term monies with it, then the bank is more likely to help in making express clearances.

(3) For very large receipts it may be worth the firm sending an employee to collect it because the delays in postage time can be very costly in the interest forgone. For example, it is often worthwhile to send an employee to a customer in the same city to collect a large receipt – this being cheaper than losing one day's interest whilst the customer's cheque is in the post.

(4) In the United States many firms have established what are known as lockboxes for collecting cheques. These have been set up because of the large delays that arise through mailing (commonly known as 'float'). They have not been utilised in Britain as of yet as the mailing system has proved to be adequate – however, any deterioration in the service or any substantial increase in postal costs may make lockboxes tenable in the United Kingdom (there is also a system of 'concentration banking', which has been built up partly because of antitrust laws in the United States, whereby banking companies cannot set up branches outside their localities; it is not relevant to the United Kingdom and nor is it likely to be in the foreseeable future).

A lockbox is a Post Office box kept in a distant location to which the firm's customers in that location send their cheques. The firm's bank or representative bank opens the box, at least daily, and transfers the funds therein to the firm's bank account by telegraphic means. Thus the day the cheque is put into the lockbox it can be received in the firm's bank account situated a considerable distance away (several thousand miles in the United States). Some reported experiences of using lockboxes have indicated that cheques received can be recorded on average about five days earlier than using the mail service. For a survey on the use of lockboxes by companies, see Mock and Shuckett.[8]

The decision whether to establish a lockbox involves a trade-off between the expenses and benefits – see Stancill.[9] The main benefit comes in the form of the interest that can be earned on the 'advanced' receipt of cash; the costs include the charges incurred in setting up the lockboxes and any charges made by the bank for operating them (this may be satisfied by keeping bank balances above a certain level). An additional factor that has to be considered is the location of them; this will involve assessing the total benefits – costs of different location strategies for lockboxes.

Another factor contributing towards the cash balance will be to take the maximum credit allowed. As far as payments go it will of course be in the interests of the firm for the mail service to be as slow as possible! In general, it will always be worthwhile to take a discount but the payment should be left until the last possible moment. When no discount is available it may be possible to settle accounts later than the due date – this should only be done if it does no damage to the firm's creditworthiness. Management will have to make subjective judgements as regards this.

The requirement for a company's technical solvency is that it has cash to meet cheques presented by creditors; there is no requirement to have cash to cover the cheque when it is drawn. Many creditors, in fact, are slow in presenting cheques and it may be a week or more before they deposit them. Some firms have tried to make use of this fact by only transferring funds out of deposit accounts or out of marketable securities in time to meet the presentation of cheques – this of course allows greater interest to be earned. Two major payments where use of the above strategy has been made is in respect of payrolls and dividends; both of these are characterised by their having many individuals each receiving smallish fractions of the total wages bill and dividend appropriation.

In order to effect this operation the payrolls and dividends are often settled out of separate bank accounts. Management draws money out of revenue-earning liquid assets and pays it into the payroll and dividend bank accounts at varying times after the cheques have been sent out. This is based upon a probability distribution of cheque presentations and the ability to borrow from the bank when there is insufficient cash.

For example, a company pays out weekly pay cheques on Friday evening of each week and so the earliest the wage earners can present their cheques is the following Monday. It is quite possible that it will be Tuesday before many of the firm's cheques start to be cleared (especially if the wage earner's bank is different from the firm's). Thus, already, we can see that the firm does not need to have all its funds in the payroll account on the Monday morning.

Additionally, some wage earners may not present their cheques until later in the week (if they have a credit balance in their own bank accounts they may well not present them until they happen to be in the vicinity of the bank, say Wednesday or Thursday). In order to quantify this behaviour a probability profile of the cheques presented on the Monday should be prepared; this may look like Fig. 4.4. Management must now specify the chance they are prepared to take of running out of cash to meet these presentations. If they are prepared to be short of cash in, say, 10 per cent of cases, then only 81 per cent of the total payroll needs to be in the payroll bank account

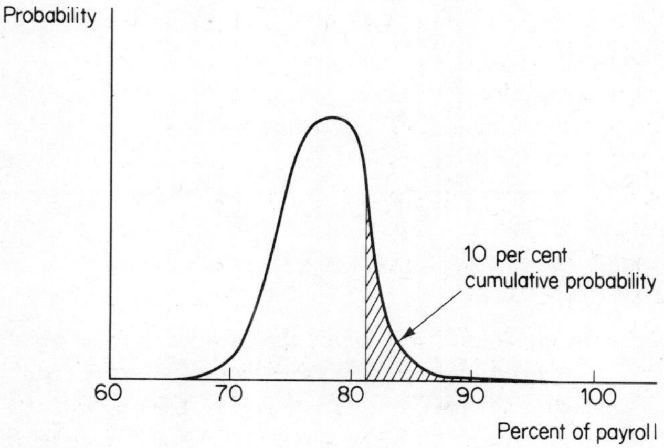

Figure 4.4

on the Monday morning. The factors influencing management's choice will be:

(*a*) their personal aversion to being short of cash; and

(*b*) the relationship with their bankers (the bank either giving short-term overdrafts or holding up the administration of handling the cheques by one day – it is very doubtful if the firm could bear the cost of wage cheques bouncing).

This type of probability analysis is then carried out for the succeeding days and the decision rule applied. We now have a profile of the cash balances needed in the payroll account; this will appear like Fig. 4.5. The potential savings by adopting such a

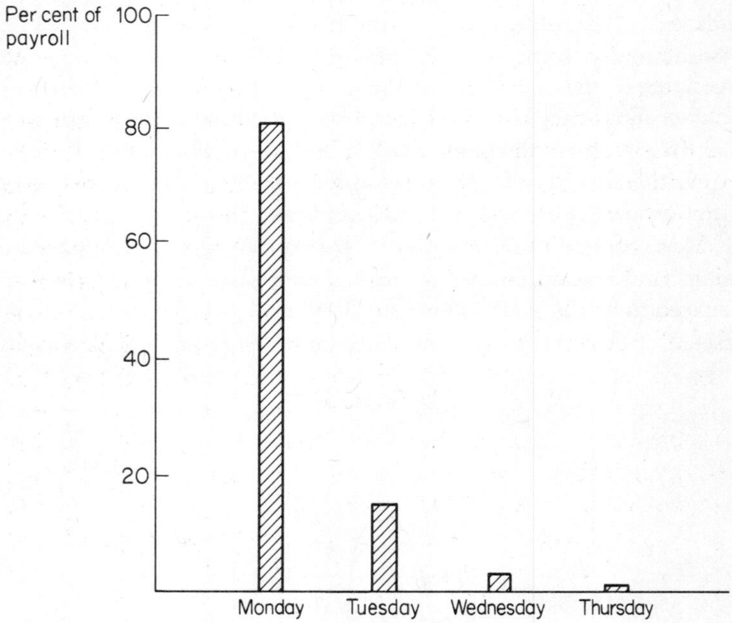

Figure 4.5

strategy can be enormous: if a firm only paid in, say, 80 per cent of its payroll by the Wednesday, the savings would be in the order of the interest earned on 20 per cent of its weekly payroll for 104 days (i.e. 52 weeks × 2 days (Monday + Tuesday)). Management must be sure of banking support in the case of shortages of cash – they could not afford cheques to bounce. The probabilistic analyses discussed above should of course be adjusted for any subjective opinions of the management as regards changing conditions. (It is also possible to adopt a conditional probability approach, i.e. the chance that a cheque will be presented on a Wednesday given that it has not been presented on the Monday or Tuesday, but this analysis requires a lot of data and is not practically feasible for most current business situations.)

This type of analysis can also be carried out on dividends. In their case, the dividend holders often take much longer than the wage earners to bank their cheques – some taking over one month and some will never present at all. The analyses can also be made for other types of payments although the non-homogeneity of the payees may make it more difficult to apply.

Management has an additional responsibility in the case of physical cash – that of its safekeeping. Retailing establishments are the obvious businesses which carry large amounts of physical cash, this can amount to as much as 10 per cent of total assets. Management must implement adequate accounting procedures to record cash-sale transactions, to carry out regular audits, to identify weaknesses in the system and to check employee honesty. Apart from the safekeeping of cash, management also needs to ensure adequate balances in the cash tills. If a cash-desk till runs out, then cash has to be quickly obtained from another till or from some central cash-desk because customers would not stand for any substantial delay. This will require additional analyses to the 'optimum cash-balance models' described earlier; various queueing models and simulation exercises can be carried out to determine optimum balances although to date virtually all stores rely solely upon experience. For a description of queueing and simulation modelling the interested reader should consult a standard operational research textbook.[10]

THE MANAGEMENT OF MARKETABLE SECURITIES

There are numerous types of marketable securities that a firm can invest in, each having characteristics which make them suitable for some investor or some requirement. The task of the company treasurer or the company's investment advisor is to select the appropriate securities to best match the requirements of the desired marketable-securities portfolio. The general requirement of holding a marketable-securities portfolio is that they can easily and quickly be converted into cash and that they earn some return. The main characteristics of marketable securities which are of interest to the firm are safety, marketability and return.

Safety refers to the principal amount of money keeping intact. Deposits with banks, local authorities and finance companies are repaid at the end of a designated period along with interest. The securities manager will, however, have to assess the creditworthiness of the depositry – during 1973, many secondary banks were forced into liquidation and only the voluntary intervention of the Bank of England saved the depositors' their money. Thus, even quite large and well-known finance companies offer some risk for deposit holders.

In the case of dated fixed-interest stocks which are sold before their maturity date, it is possible they will gain or lose value over even short periods of time (the market price is an inverse function of interest rates – if interest rates went up we would expect the market price of the security to fall). The reduction in value during short periods of time should not be too great as interest rates rarely move more than say 1 per cent in a week; however, some up or down movement can be expected. What is important is whether the dated securities are repaid – this uncertainty is not present in U.K. Government Stocks (Gilt edged) but could occur with industrial companies.

Ordinary stocks and shares offer considerable risk as to their values although a well-constructed portfolio of them should reduce the uncertainties surrounding the expected outcome. Investing in ordinary stocks and shares, if at all, will generally form a long-term component of the marketable-securities portfolio. Additionally, it will depend upon the investment manager's success in investing in equity shares (the Board of Directors is unlikely to give the manager authority to invest in equities if his record has been poor).

Marketability relates to the ease of selling securities, measured in terms of the length of time it takes to sell the security once a sale decision has been taken, the time taken for the proceeds to arrive and the degree of fall in market price that may have to be accepted for a quick sale (this applies mainly to equities). The time it takes to sell a security depends upon:

(1) *The market place.* In the United Kingdom there is a fairly sophisticated Stock Exchange where equities and both dated and

undated fixed-interest stocks can be traded. However, if a particular security is a small issue (e.g. a quoted company with a market capitalisation under £1 million), then it is possible that a deal could take a number of days if a 'reasonable' price is to be obtained.

(2) *The percentage of a particular security held.* If, for example, an investor owned 40 per cent of a quoted company's equity, it is doubtful if a sale of the whole amount could be made on the day of the disposal decision – it may take several weeks to offload the shares or to arrange a special sale.

The extent to which a price may fall upon a quick sale is likely to be largely a function of the percentage of an issue held; the emphasis being on equity shares. Unless very large amounts of fixed-interest stocks were sold (i.e. several hundred million) it is doubtful if prices would be marked down substantially. The major rule to follow as far as marketability goes is to invest in relatively large issues (with a market capitalisation of say £5 million), and as regards equities to invest only smallish percentages in each individual security (say 1 per cent of that security's equity).

As regards the time of payment for a sale, the proceeds from a sale of British Government, corporation, public board and Commonwealth stocks are normally for settlement on the business day following the day of the bargain; for other stocks and for equity shares the proceeds of sale are made on twenty-four days (roughly equidistant) in the year. (For a description of the Stock Exchange dealing mechanism see Cooper and Cridlan[11]). There may be some fair time delay between a sale and the receipt of the proceeds (in the case of a three-week account it could be as much as twenty-nine days). However, if the amounts are large and the relationships with the broker are good then an advance payment or a loan against the sale proceeds may be made by the broker; in addition, the firm's banks may make advances against sale contract notes unless the money situation is extremely tight.

As regards deposits, these are made for fixed time periods. It is often possible to negotiate an early termination of the deposit but this may be costly (i.e. forgoing some part of the interest) and in any case it is entirely at the discretion of the depositry. Sometimes, bank loans can be obtained against the security of a deposit account but this is likely to be expensive as interest-payable rates generally exceed interest-received rates.

The longer that money can be left on deposit (especially liquid resources being built up for some major expenditure) the greater the interest rate it will attract. However, in deciding the term length of deposit account to open, management has to be very sure about the duration of its surplus cash flows; in addition, knowing the duration of surplus cash flows also allows a better selection of dated fixed-interest stocks, as those maturing on the appropriate dates can be selected. By making a detailed cash-flow statement (possibly daily), management will have estimates of how long varying amounts of cash may be available and so the choice of investments can be made accordingly.

The return on an investment refers to the after-tax total of interest, dividends and capital appreciation (depreciation). For deposit accounts, the amount of return is known exactly as is the case for dated stocks that are held to maturity; for dated fixed-interest stocks not held to maturity and for undated fixed-interest stocks, the capital gain–loss will not be known with certainty – market prices being a function of future interest rates. Equity shares provide the most volatile of returns as over the long term they are associated with uncertain profits and in the short term they are influenced by a host of logical and illogical factors.

Generally speaking, the higher the expected return offered by a security the greater the risk, and thus managers have to trade-off their risk aversion with the higher expected returns; additionally, longer-term investments and deposits tend to attract slightly higher interest rates. Thus the choice between securities partly depends upon the investment manager's strength of views of the returns on securities and on the degree of risk reduction that may be obtained by diversifying within a security class or into several classes of investment.

The efficient diversifying of securities can be approached by mean–variance portfolio theory.[12,13] This produces an 'efficient set' of portfolios (where the expected returns are maximised for given levels of risk) which are then matched with the investor's risk–return indifference curves. Portfolio theory requires a lot of data and so little application has been made in the U.K. up to the present, managers generally diversifying across industry groupings (for an equity portfolio).

The main criteria for the construction of a marketable-securities and deposit-account portfolio are:

(1) For the optimal cash balance as calculated on pages 82 and 85, very liquid assets should be held which have a fixed principal or whose values change very little. In effect, this may mean investing money overnight in the money market or by buying Government securities.

(2) For known future expenses, i.e. weekly or monthly wage bills, a security can be chosen which matures at the appropriate payment date. Scope also exists for investment in gilt-edged securities and in longer-term deposit accounts. It is doubtful if other fixed-interest securities or equity shares would be worth purchasing unless they were held for well over one month (unless in the case of equities the investment manager had some special information). In order to assess the timing and appropriateness of longer-term investments a fairly detailed cash budget is required.

(3) If investments in company securities (i.e. equity shares, loans, stocks, debentures) are made, then consideration should be given to diversification; additionally, not more than a small part (say 1 per cent) of a security's total issue should be acquired. Deposit accounts with secondary banks or with financial companies often offer higher interest; however, they are also more risky and so again diversification should be considered.

(4) If investments of large amounts are made, even in Government securities, then some diversification will be needed to prevent holding a large percentage of one particular issue.

(5) In dealing with the money market it will pay to obtain expert advice. If the average interest rate on average surplus funds of say £1 million could be raised from 10 to 10·25 per cent this would provide additional interest of £25,000p.a. Thus an expert investment executive should be employed or the detailed advice of a stockbroker or banker obtained (they may do it free if they get all the firm's business or, in the case of the bank, the bank account).

MAJOR SHORT-TERM INVESTMENT OPPORTUNITIES

Deposits

There are various types of deposit accounts in which a firm can invest its surplus cash, offering varying returns and maturity dates. The major depositries are described below; except where otherwise stated the interest rates on the deposit vary in line with the currently prevailing interest rates.

The Money Market. For companies with substantial amounts of cash (say £10,000 or over) there is a sophisticated market whereby money can be lent overnight and interest earned. Banks and various finance companies require such monies on a daily basis to balance their cash accounts and maintain certain ratios. Because of the wide compass of the money market, most firms with overnight surplus cash will use the services of a merchant bank or stockbroker in investing.

Deposit Accounts with Banks. The normal bank deposit account requires seven days' notice of withdrawal. If immediate cash is required it might be possible to draw cash quicker but this may mean no interest being earned. Merchant banks, acceptance houses, discount houses and major finance companies (i.e. hire-purchase companies) also offer time-period deposit accounts; some of these may insist on minimum deposits of, say, £10,000 upwards. The longer the agreed period of the deposit the greater will be the interest rate.

Deposits and Loans with Local Authorities. Investments can be made with local authorities for varying periods; there is usually a minimum sum to be deposited (often £10,000). Although some local-authority stocks are negotiable, the market is very small and so the firm should ensure that the cash is surplus for all of the minimum period of deposit. The interest rate is fixed at the date of the issue (deposits may carry a varying interest rate).

Sterling Certificates of Deposit (*S.C.D.*). This is a negotiable certificate issued by a bank and thus it has a market value as with other dated fixed-interest stocks. A certificate is for a minimum amount of £50,000 and a maximum amount of £250,000 and has a life of three months to five years. There is an active market for S.C.D.s and so certificates can be bought with just a few days to maturity; they carry a fixed rate of interest.

Fixed-interest stocks

These can be divided into those that have a fixed date for repayment and those that do not (these are in the minority – the best known being 3½ per cent War Loan). Many are issued by the Government and because of their backing they are referred to as gilt-edged. Other fixed-interest stocks are issued by foreign governments and by commercial companies (often referred to as loan stocks and debentures). These latter types need to be appraised carefully as to their creditworthiness: the more risky they are, the greater the returns that are offered.

Table 4.3 Money-market rates (as at 10 December 1975)

Bank of England Minimum Lending Rate $11\frac{1}{2}$%
(Last changed 28/11/75)
Clearing Banks Base Rate 11%
Discount Mkt Loans%
Overnight: Open 11 Close $8\frac{1}{2}$
Week Fixed: $10\frac{3}{4}$–$10\frac{7}{8}$

	Treasury Bills (Dis%)		
Buying		Selling	
2 months	$10\frac{7}{8}$	2 months	$10\frac{27}{32}$
3 months	$10\frac{15}{16}$	3 months	$10\frac{7}{8}$
	Prime Bank Bills (Dis%)	Trades (Dis%)	
2 months	$10\frac{15}{16}$–$10\frac{7}{8}$	3 months	$11\frac{1}{2}$
3 months	$10\frac{15}{16}$–$10\frac{7}{8}$	4 months	$11\frac{5}{8}$
4 months	$10\frac{15}{16}$–$10\frac{13}{16}$	6 months	$11\frac{7}{8}$
6 months	$10\frac{15}{16}$–$10\frac{13}{16}$		
	Local Authority Bonds		
1 month	$11\frac{1}{4}$–11	7 months	$11\frac{3}{8}$–$11\frac{1}{2}$
2 months	$11\frac{3}{8}$–$11\frac{1}{8}$	8 months	$11\frac{3}{8}$–$11\frac{1}{2}$
3 months	$11\frac{3}{8}$–$11\frac{1}{2}$	9 months	$11\frac{5}{8}$–$11\frac{3}{8}$
4 months	$11\frac{3}{8}$–$11\frac{1}{2}$	10 months	$11\frac{5}{8}$–$11\frac{3}{8}$
5 months	$11\frac{3}{8}$–$11\frac{1}{2}$	11 months	$11\frac{5}{8}$–$11\frac{3}{8}$
6 months	$11\frac{3}{8}$–$11\frac{1}{2}$	12 months	$11\frac{5}{8}$–$11\frac{3}{8}$
	Secondary Mkt. £CD Rates (%)		
1 month	$10\frac{15}{16}$–$10\frac{13}{16}$	6 months	$11\frac{3}{16}$–$11\frac{1}{4}$
3 months	$11\frac{1}{8}$–11	12 months	$11\frac{3}{8}$–$11\frac{1}{8}$
	Local Authority Market (%)		
2 days	$10\frac{3}{4}$	3 months	$11\frac{1}{4}$
7 days	11	6 months	$11\frac{3}{8}$
1 month	11	1 year	$12\frac{1}{8}$
	Interbank Market (%)		
Overnight: Open	$10\frac{3}{8}$–$10\frac{5}{8}$	Close	$10\frac{3}{8}$–$10\frac{5}{8}$
1 week	$10\frac{7}{8}$–$10\frac{3}{4}$	6 months	$11\frac{1}{4}$–$11\frac{3}{16}$
1 month	$10\frac{15}{16}$–$10\frac{13}{16}$	9 months	$11\frac{5}{16}$–$11\frac{3}{16}$
3 months	$11\frac{1}{8}$–11	12 months	$11\frac{5}{8}$–$11\frac{1}{2}$
	First Class Finance Houses (Mkt. Rate%)		
3 months	$11\frac{5}{8}$	6 months	$11\frac{11}{16}$

Finance House Base Rate 12%

Table 4.4 *U.K. security yields* (per cent per annum, except for index number in right-hand column)

	Government stocks				Company securities				
					Bank of England index		FT-Actuaries indices		
	Short-dated (5 years)	Medium-dated (10 years)	Long-dated (20 years)	$3\frac{1}{2}$% War Loan	High-coupon debenture and loan stocks	20-year debenture and loan stocks	Industrial ordinary shares (500 shares)		
Last working days	Calculated redemption yields			Flat yield	Redemption yield	Redemption yield	Dividend yield	Earnings yield	Price index (10 April 1962=100)
1974 Jan	12·87	13·48	13·43	13·33	13·96	14·20	5·37	12·42	142·8
Feb	12·54	13·25	13·37	13·47	14·26	14·64	5·14	12·44	149·6
Mar	13·45	14·28	14·48	14·69	15·45	15·85	6·47	17·71	120·4
Apr	12·32	13·68	14·25	14·60	14·99	15·77	6·23	16·76	131·0
May	11·57	13·08	13·62	13·74	14·51	15·20	6·76	18·87	120·4
June	13·26	14·67	15·29	15·37	15·98	16·83	7·56	21·14	107·8
July	12·09	14·23	14·98	15·12	15·95	16·46	8·02	22·66	101·8
Aug	12·92	14·73	15·49	15·75	16·60	17·14	9·09	25·86	89·8
Sep	11·82	14·07	14·89	15·01	16·53	17·18	10·59	29·66	78·7
Oct	12·12	15·28	16·59	17·07	17·85	18·51	10·20	28·57	81·9
Nov	13·00	15·94	16·75	16·73	18·62	19·36	12·08	[illegible]	[illegible]
[illegible]	[illegible]	[illegible]	[illegible]	[illegible]	[illegible]	[illegible]	[illegible]	[illegible]	[illegible]

1975 Jan	11·23	13·61	14·98	15·05	16·03	17·21	7·70	22·33	103·7
Feb	11·21	13·08	14·31	14·48	15·11	16·10	6·52	19·06	127·7
Mar	10·55	12·05	13·34	13·68	14·22	14·80	7·03	20·57	119·6
Apr	11·22	13·20	14·85	15·19	15·60	15·82	6·31	19·59	139·0
May	11·04	13·21	14·45	14·67	15·52	16·05	5·95	18·57	147·4
June	11·30	13·15	14·57	14·77	15·68	15·98	6·76	20·73	131·1
July	11·77	12·84	13·88	14·06	14·85	15·47	7·03	21·51	126·8
Aug	11·61	12·73	13·79	13·87	14·78	15·38	6·19	18·68	144·6
Sep	11·71	12·92	14·11	14·17	14·46	15·29	6·12	16·39	148·8
Oct	12·26	13·68	14·83	14·73	15·47	16·06	5·90	15·68	155·3
Nov	12·17	13·71	14·83	14·74	15·41	15·93	5·83	15·23	158·5

Source: *Bank of England Quarterly Bulletin*, 15, 4 (December 1975).

Table 4.5 *Selected liquid assets of industrial and commercial companies*

Amounts outstanding
End of period

£ million

	Treasury bills	Tax reserve certificates	Tax deposit accounts	Local authority temporary debt	Deposits with banking sector			Deposits with building societies	Deposits with finance houses	Total identified	Bank advances	
					Deposit banks	Others	Negotiable certificates of deposit				Deposit banks	Others
1974 1st quarter	36	12	6	519	3658	4542	849	149	133	9804	8216	7207
2nd quarter	36	9	7	509	3697	4495	705	149	140	9747	8795	7977
3rd quarter	154	8	12	518	4196	4335	611	149	104	10087	8952	8435
4th quarter	81	7	13	484	4517	4052	469	149	97	9869	9123	8896
1975 1st quarter	51	3	4	424	4404	4464	468	149	114	10081	9353	8963

Source: Central Statistical Office.

In the case of dated stocks the return consists of both the annual interest rate and the difference between the market price and the redemption price. Major fixed-interest securities are very marketable and their prices fluctuate according to the movements in the general level of interest rates.

Treasury Bills. These are issued by the Government with a normal maturity date of 91 days. Companies can buy these bills via their banks.

Ordinary stocks and shares (equities)

These are marketable securities but, unlike the prior mentioned investments, their values fluctuate considerably; hence it is unusual for short-term surplus cash to be invested in equities. If such investments are made, then a portfolio of several different equities should be built up so as to reduce the risk (possibly units in a unit trust or shares in an investment trust should be bought).

The above represent the major short-term investment opportunities available to firms with surplus funds. In general, higher expected interest rates and returns will be received from:

(*a*) longer-term commitments of money, i.e. longer-term deposits; and

(*b*) more risky investments and deposits.

Table 4.3 shows the prevailing money-market rates at 10 December 1975. Table 4.4 shows selected security yields on U.K. issues and Table 4.5 shows selected liquid assets of industrial and commercial companies.

CHAPTER 5

Short-Term Financing of Working Capital

Figs. 1.2, 1.3, 1.4 and 1.5 showed a typical asset structure of a firm and of its possible financing. Using long-term finance solely is the most conservative as regards the certainty of finance but it is probably the most costly in terms of interest rates and in creating surplus cash. At the other extreme, using solely short-term finance runs the risk of the finance not being renewed and of the very possible consequent bankruptcy. Short-term relates to finance that is typically repayable within one year; medium and long-term finance is that which typically extends beyond one year, e.g. debentures, preference shares, ordinary shares, retained earnings. In between these two extremes lie a host of financing strategies which a company can adopt. One, which was depicted in Fig. 1.3, is to finance the permanent segment of the current assets by long-term capital and the fluctuating current assets by short-term capital; of course, this involves recognising the 'permanent' element of current assets. In practice, most firms adopt a policy of financing some part of their current assets by long-term finance; the traditional textbook solution is that one-half should be financed in this way (the current ratio being 2·0; this ratio is described in Chapter 6). Specific industries have variations on these figures of course.

The choice of the financing policy will be influenced by the following:

(1) Creditors and the capital markets often set broad limits on the financing policies of current assets for specific industries. Firms may find it difficult and expensive to stray from the norm.

(2) The state of the capital and lending markets. If, say, the capital markets are in a depressed state, as often happens for periods of up to two years, then short-term finance may have to be used even if this violates management's 'optimum' policy.

(3) The make-up of current assets and of outside markets; for example, food retailers may be able to rely heavily upon short-term financing as they have quickly realisable inventories.

(4) The extent and methods of recent increases in financing; for example, if there has been a good deal of recent capital expenditure financed by long-term loans, then firms may be forced to finance increases in current assets by short-term means alone.

(5) Management's attitudes towards the riskiness involved with the different forms of financing. This will involve management preparing cash budgets, profit and loss and balance-sheet forecasts. From these, the need for, and the dates of, future finance can be estimated and, by making judgements on the capital markets and the banking situations, subjective opinions on financing can be obtained.

Risks Involved with Long-term Financing

The risk involved with raising long-term finance is that it might only be employed for a short period of time (e.g. a seasonal peak in inventories); the remainder of the time it will be invested in marketable securities and, whilst this will earn a return, it will not usually be as much as the interest being paid out (unless the marketable securities are risky when the returns may be high). It is often possible to repay the loan early (or in the case of quoted debenture stock to purchase them in the stock market) but this is at the discretion of the lender and often incurs penalty costs or high terminal-interest charges. The interest rate on long-term finance during stable periods usually exceeds that on short-term loans; during a temporary period of abnormally high interest rates, however, this differential may disappear altogether. Another cost that will have to be incurred is that involved in raising the finance (in the case of debentures this may include underwriting fees, Stock Exchange fees, printing expenses); these costs are more expensive than those relating to short-term finance although short-term finance will probably have to be raised more often!

Risks Involved with Short-term Financing

The risk involved with short-term finance is that it might not be renewed. In certain cases this can lead to bankruptcy (where the fixed and/or current assets are slow to realise) which would otherwise have been averted (if financed by long-term capital). Even if bankruptcy does not ensue, it may mean the firm operating at far below its potential as pessimistic bankers and creditors reduce their support. The withdrawal or reduction of short-term finance is fairly common, occurring every few years as the economy turns down and as the Government of the day adopts a tight money policy. Another risk is that the rate of interest for many types of short-term finance are not known beyond the current date (e.g. overdraft rates vary with the Bank Rate); although these are as likely to turn down as to move up, the existence of the uncertainty makes it difficult to plan.

Choice of Short-term Finance

Once having decided to finance with short-term funds, the firm is now left with selecting the appropriate type of short-term finance. There are many sources and the aim of this chapter is to discuss the characteristics of the major types. As will be seen some sources (e.g. factoring) are specific to certain assets; it will also be noticed that some of the sources are of a revolving nature (often contractually so) and thus have some degree of permanency attached to them (up to, say, two years). Detailed descriptions of long-term financing methods are not within the scope of working capital and are not dealt with here but, for a coverage of the sources and the selection of long- and medium-term finance, see Midgley and Burns.[1]

TRADE CREDIT

The most important source of short-term finance is trade credit and this being especially so for smaller firms (see Table 1.2). Trade credit represents goods and services (including electricity, rent, telephone and wage expenses) received by the firm for which payment is made later – if fortunate, this may be after the sale of the finished goods. Suppliers often give credit terms to the firm – that is payment is not made until, say, 30 days after purchase; this especially applies in business between firms, there being little ordinary credit given to individuals (who mainly receive credit in the form of hire-purchase and instalment schemes). The extent of this trade credit (which represents accounts receivable of the supplier) depends upon the trade custom, the type of goods involved and the financial positions of the supplier and the purchaser (i.e. suppliers who are short of cash are unlikely to grant credit; healthy suppliers may be prepared to extend more generous credit terms to long-standing customers and especially those in temporary financial trouble).

Trade credit is also a very convenient source of finance as it accrues immediately a purchase is made and, further, is an informal way of receiving credit – no requests have to be made. Apart from credit impairment by taking excessive time before paying and apart from discounts lost, trade credit is free and thus the most desirable type of short-term finance. If a discount is allowed by the supplier, however, it will probably pay the firm to take advantage of this. As shown in Chapter 3, these discounts are usually quite generous, e.g. the terms 2/10, *N*/30 represent an annual interest rate of 36 per cent. Not taking this discount, therefore, involves an opportunity cost of 36 per cent, and it is doubtful if the firm could employ the funds for 20 days to obtain a return earning 36 per cent per annum.

If a discount is not available or if the discount period has passed, then the firm should take as much credit as possible. Table 5.1 shows

Table 5.1

Terms of sale 2/10, *N*/30

Implicit per annum interest cost if paid at the end of the following number of days.

Days		Interest per annum per cent
30	$\frac{2}{98} \times \frac{365}{20}$	37·2
60	$\frac{2}{98} \times \frac{365}{50}$	14·9
90	$\frac{2}{98} \times \frac{365}{80}$	9·3
120	$\frac{2}{98} \times \frac{365}{110}$	6·8

the cost of taking a discount and paying after 30 days, 60 days, 90 days and 120 days. Clearly, the longer the time before payment the less the 'opportunity cost'. The caveat to taking more credit than that allowed is that it can lead to credit impairment and poor relations with suppliers of goods and services. The ramifications of these were discussed in Chapter 4 and include the losing of supplies, slowness in delivery and poor service. The assessment of how much extended credit can be taken is subjective and depends upon the individual circumstances. Whilst the extension of credit is sound practice it can be taken too far; experience and judgement is therefore required. The taking of maximum credit applies equally to services as well as purchases of goods; for example, getting the employees to receive their pay monthly (in arrears) as opposed to weekly lowers the true wages cost (up to a month's credit being given). Additionally, tax planning can help in reducing current cash outflows; there is usually scope for delaying tax payments at the time of a change-around of the tax structure, as happened with the introduction of Advanced Corporation Tax.

For specific contract work such as that carried out by civil engineers and engineering firms, it is quite common for the firm to receive progress payments in respect of the work completed to date. Occasionally this is extended with firms obtaining a payment from the customer in advance of work done. These payments cut down the need for finance and every effort should be made to reach such an arrangement with the customer. Additionally, customers sometimes supply the raw materials and components to the firm and, in this case, the firm is relieved of substantial financing and only incurs costs in respect of the conversion of the raw materials into the finished products. Again, this practice is mainly prevalent in civil engineering and engineering industries but there is no reason why, with reasoned planning, it cannot be developed for other trades.

BANK OVERDRAFTS

Bank overdraft facilities consist of an agreed line of credit on which the firm can draw current-account cheques. Technically, the overdraft is repayable at call but, in practice, banks normally give some specified longer time period such as 6 or 12 months within which the firm must eliminate the overdraft or reduce it to a lower level. The period of the overdraft is usually arranged in conjunction with the cash requirements of the firm; for example, seasonal businesses such as agriculture, or as bridging finance where, say, a payment has to be made for a new office block before the proceeds of the sale of the old one have been received.

In the majority of cases, the overdraft will be renewable (known as revolving) where, subject to various factors, the bank will be willing to allow what are, in effect, permanent overdrafts (note that the bank still has the right to recall the overdraft straight away – thus 'permanent' overdraft facilities are not 100 per cent certain). Banks will also give long-term standby facilities where they agree to the overdraft rising to a certain level for short periods of time. Examples might include import–export dealers who might have to pay, say, home-based suppliers before the ultimate foreign buyer pays, and stockbrokers who may need finance to cover various short-term transactions. The major factors that the bank will look at in considering the renewal of an overdraft are the same as those relating to new customers, referred to below, and of course to the firm's past behaviour with its overdraft facilities.

In assessing an approach for overdraft facilities the bank will want to know:

(1) The maximum facility required, for what purposes and when and how it will be repaid. The firm will therefore have to prepare detailed cash-flow budgets and profits forecasts.

(2) The current financial position of the firm and its recent past performance. This will require audited accounts over the past five years and these will be analysed along the lines discussed in Chapter 6. The bank may also request additional financial information.

(3) What security can be offered. Over half of bank overdrafts are now secured and firms requiring large facilities must expect to be asked to provide security, this often being a general floating charge over the firm's assets. Additionally, in the case of small firms the bank may require a personal guarantee from the principal directors or partners, thus making them liable if the firm itself is unable to repay.

Apart from the above conditions that have to be satisfied, an overdraft also depends upon the availability of cash in the banking sector. During the recent past, banks have had at various times to cut back on even existing overdraft commitments; thus, even if the firm is very sound it may find it impossible to obtain an overdraft if there is strong credit restriction.

The bank may specify a repayment schedule that has to be kept to. In conjunction with the firm's cash-flow forecasts presented to him, the banker will work out an overdraft limit for each period. If, during the course of events, the firm finds some delay in building up cash then they should communicate this information to the bank. The bank may also impose other conditions on the firm; major examples include a current asset liquidation programme and the maintaining of various gearing and solvency ratios.

It is very important to build up a rapport with the bank and especially with the individual managers. Although various asset ratios and profitability trends may be formally stipulated by the bank, the granting, and the level, of overdraft facilities are largely a matter of personal judgement by the bank's officers. In building up a good banking relationship it will help considerably if the firm speedily and fully informs the bank of any unexpected changes in the cash-flow situation; this will also enable the bank to give any advice it can on the adoption of some strategy to ameliorate the liquidity position.

The interest rate on bank overdrafts is normally of the order of 1 or 2 per cent above the prevailing base rate (which is set by the banks themselves – this will be competitive with other banks, however). Sometimes a bank may charge a higher interest if the loan is risky; additionally, a commitment fee or some other expense is often charged by the bank for opening an overdraft account and for giving standby credit. The interest rate varies with the prevailing base rate and is charged on the outstanding balance in the current account; it is an allowable expense for taxation and thus reduces the firm's tax charge. Generally, overdrafts are one of the cheapest sources of finance and should be used in preference to other loans.

LOANS BY BANKS AND OTHER FINANCIAL ORGANISATIONS

Banks and financial companies (discount houses, merchant banks, investment trusts, pension funds) often give time-period loans to firms. These are differentiated from overdrafts in that they are for a specified period (say three months to five years) and that a principal sum is borrowed (if all of this is not needed by the firm then they have to invest it). Often the interest rate is fixed or semi-fixed at the beginning of the loan. Whether taking a fixed-interest loan is better than taking a variable-interest loan depends on the movement of future interest rates. The credit assessment for banking loans is usually more stringent than for overdrafts and security will almost certainly be required. They are very useful when used to finance a particular asset or project as the timings can be matched; additionally, the money market may be able to lend money to the company on a daily or weekly basis to cover short-term cash deficits. Bank loans tend to be slightly more expensive than overdrafts and are not as easily obtained; however, they are a fairly important source of finance. For large companies and especially for those with overseas branches, the International Money Market provides a substantial source of finance, the major short-term source being perhaps Euro dollars for which there exists a sophisticated market. For details of international finance see a specialised text such as Einzig.[2]

BILL FINANCING – BILLS OF EXCHANGE

This provides a method of financing purchases and sales and involves the borrower undertaking to pay a particular sum of money at some specified future date. If a financial company 'accepts' the bill (for which it receives a commission) it undertakes to meet that bill at maturity if the drawer of the bill defaults; there are a number of these companies who specialise in bills of exchange. By having the bill accepted by a respectable finance house makes it a very marketable security. If the bill is not 'accepted', then the drawer will have to have an impeccable record and reputation if it is to use trade bills in settlement of its debts.

Trade bills are drawn by the purchaser promising to pay for the goods at a specific future date – often as far ahead as three or six months. The seller is willing to take the bill in settlement if it has been 'accepted' or if the purchaser is completely creditworthy, and can then sell the bill in the money market (this is usually known as 'discounting the bill').

Acceptance credits occur when a purchaser draws a bill on an accepting house (a financial institution) and sells it in the money market. The proceeds from this sale are then used to pay the seller; the acceptance house is repaid later.

Trade bills and acceptance credits give medium-term finance for firms: they buy goods now and pay for them in, say, six months' time. Of course, any supplier agreeing to receive a bill may charge a slightly higher price to cover the interest that could have been earned on an immediate cash settlement. Additionally, the acceptance house will require a fee for its guarantee on the bill and it may also impose some financial conditions on the firm for providing a revolving 'acceptance' of bills. In accepting a bill, the acceptance house will of course have to make the usual investigations of the firm's creditworthiness – similar to the analyses carried out by banks in granting overdrafts.

Bill financing has traditionally been associated with export selling where the purchaser is not prepared to pay cash until he has inspected the goods, which may take up to, say, two months to arrive from the supplier. The supplier meantime requires payment – by receiving a bill he can discount this and receive cash. Bills of exchange are traditionally used for largish sales and so are generally not too appropriate for firms making many sales of small amounts.

Firms that receive trade bills in settlement of a sale can discount them immediately or at any time before maturity to obtain cash. It is important, however, that the bill has been accepted by a reputable finance house or is drawn upon a well-known, financially-sound company. The rate of discount is usually about 1 per cent or so higher than base rate; for example, a firm receives a £200 bill payable in three months' time; it discounts the bill straight away with its bankers receiving £196. The firm has therefore surrendered £4 in receiving £196 now, representing an annual interest rate of 8·4 per cent, i.e. $(4/196) = 2{\cdot}04$ per cent discount in the period of three months; on an annual basis this is equivalent to $(1{\cdot}0204)^4 - 1 = 8{\cdot}4$ per cent.

FACTORING OF DEBTS

As briefly described in Chapter 3, many finance companies offer a factoring service where they give either a loan against the security of debts or actually buy the debts from the firm. This provides a very valuable source of finance for the firm; they have to grant credit terms because of competitive pressures and factoring gives them one source of finance for doing so. There are a number of different types of factoring service and all these alternatives are often provided by a single finance house. Amongst the major types are:

(1) Where the factor acquires the debts, agrees to take the bad debts that may arise (for which the factor may insist on the firm taking out credit insurance) and undertakes the administrative work. This is a complete service and the firm need have no more worry. It is the most expensive type although cost savings are effected by taking away the administration and the bad-debts expense.

(2) Modifications to the above where the bad-debts expense could be arranged so that only part of it will be suffered by the factor; this makes the firm adopt a sensible attitude in selecting credit customers.

(3) The factor could give an advance against the debts with the firm doing its own debt collection. An advantage of the firm doing

its own administrative work is that its customers will not be aware of the factoring (sometimes known as confidential invoice discounting), this being thought by many to be a sign of financial weakness.

The service is effected by the factor paying some percentage (say 80 to 90 per cent) of the debts to the firm immediately. The debtors eventually pay either the factor or the firm (confidential invoice discounting), the latter remitting the proceeds to the factor. At this stage some balancing may be required – possibly the factor sending the firm the balance of the debts (say 10 to 20 per cent), less their commission.

The service can be provided on the whole of the debtors (in which case the firm may have to bear any bad debts) or on debts selected by the factor. Some factors provide a continuous revolving service where they automatically provide finance at the time of sale.

Factors provide a very valuable service to firms and this especially applies during periods of rapidly expanding sales. Their services are not cheap, however, bank-overdraft facilities being much less expensive (although they do not offer administrative services). In appraising whether and what type of factoring service to use management should incorporate all the above considerations. By a careful analysis of the costs involved, and of the alternative sources of finance and of potential investment opportunities that exist, the firm should be able to reach the optimum solution for that period; further analyses will have to be made for future periods to account for changing circumstances.

SUBSIDIARY FINANCE COMPANIES

Some firms set up separate finance subsidiaries to which all the debts are transferred (factored). This especially applies where the group as a whole sells a wide range of differing goods. By setting up a finance subsidiary, a specialised team of credit managers can be built up, along with a sophisticated debt-collection service. Perhaps the main reason for setting up the subsidiary, however, is that it may enable greater amounts of long-term fixed-interest borrowings to be obtained (this assumes the capital market gives higher ratios to finance companies). This in turn may reduce the group's overall cost of capital, a complex term but one which relates to the rate of return that investors expect (require) the particular firm to make. For a discussion of the cost of capital see Lewellen.[3]

HIRE PURCHASE AND LEASING

These forms of finance are available for the acquisition of medium-term and long-term assets and do not apply to short-term assets such as inventories and debtors. However, financing longer-term assets by these methods does relieve the strain on working capital by reducing present cash outflows, and it is for this reason that hire purchase and lease financing are sometimes included in texts on working capital. However, longer-term asset financing is not really in the realm of working capital and so no description and analysis is given here; the interested reader should consult Midgley and Burns, reference to which was made earlier.

THE USE OF INVENTORY AS SECURITY

Another possible source of finance is to use the firm's inventory as security for a loan. This has been developed quite extensively in the United States but has received much less recognition in the U.K. There are a number of ways in which the loan can operate, for example: (1) making a loan of, say, 80 per cent of the cost price of the inventories; (2) making a loan against specific inventories (e.g. a particular finished product); (3) the lender being paid directly by the debtor arising from the sale of the inventory; (4) the lender only allowing the inventory to be sold against the repayment of his loan (a bank or credit factor providing the finance). Within these procedures there are numerous modifications to suit particular requirements. In time, this form of financing could become very popular in the U.K. and could be conducted on a revolving basis. Apart from the specific mortgaging of inventory, a general charge over it is often applied by banks and other lenders when they take out a floating charge over all the firm's assets.

Model-building Approaches in Selecting Sources of Finance

The main criteria in selecting the appropriate finance for working capital are cheapness and the maturity structure. In considering the cheapness some regard must be had for the impact on the firm's cost of capital; it may be that although the finance raised is cheap it could make the firm more risky; for a discussion of the concept and measurement of the cost of capital see Lewellen, to whom a reference was made above. This is almost universally conducted on a subjective basis but some researchers have shown that objective optimal financing solutions can be obtained. Robichek, Teichroew and Jones,[4] for example, reduced the problem of financing cash deficits and investing cash surpluses into a linear program. Their method involved preparing a future cash budget which showed periods of cash deficits and cash surpluses. The manager is then faced with various methods of financing or investing the balances, and each of these methods involves costs and constraints (for example, the factoring of debts cannot amount to any more than the face value of the debts). The objective function of the L.P. was how to provide the funds required, as shown by the cash budget, at the minimum total cost. Within the constraints set, the solution to the L.P. produced an optimum financing strategy for the period under review. Although Robichek *et al*'s model had to use various assumptions, it pointed out the possible application of operational research techniques to the solution of financing problems. In time, and with greater research, these methods may become very viable for all sizes of firms.

Summary

This chapter has outlined the major sources of short-term finance; the cheapest is trade credit followed by bank overdrafts. The extent of the credit given by these sources depends very much on the firm's past relationships with the creditor and banker and on the record of profitability and the net worth of the business. Other money loans are likely to be more expensive and given on more onerous terms; they will also be more difficult to acquire in spite of these conditions. Factoring is a well-established source of funds but is limited to the balance on the accounts receivable; this is usually quite large, however! The specific pledging of inventory is a much less well-developed form of finance but it is at the same time the one with the greatest potential. Both factoring and inventory pledging will be more expensive than bank overdrafts but, in the case of factoring, it is a readily available source. In determining the optimum mix of short-term finance the firm should go for the cheapest source first, unless there are any specific conditions attached to this which make it more onerous in other terms.

Table 1.2 showed that trade and other creditors formed the major source of short-term finance and this accounted for almost three times as much as bank overdrafts. Bills of exchange and loans from the money market forms only a small amount of total short-term finance; factoring is likewise a small source of finance but has been growing rapidly in recent years. It is unlikely that the above situation will change greatly in the near future although significant growth is expected in factor finance.

CHAPTER 6

The Analysis of Working-Capital Positions by Outsiders

The component items of, and the overall position of, working capital is analysed by outside parties for credit extension, lending and investment purposes. Interested parties include:

(1) *Trade and expense creditors who give short-term credit to the firm.* They only give credit as long as they think the firm will settle the debt on the due date.

(2) *Overdrafts and loans by banking and financial institutions.* The granting of these facilities, the amounts involved, the conditions attached, the security involved and the interest rates will all depend on the institution's opinion of the firm's creditworthiness.

(3) *Finance extended by credit factors.* The extent of their charges will be partly dependent upon their assessment of the time it is taking debtors to pay and the bad-debts expense.

(4) *Pledging of inventory as security for a loan.* The lender will want to make an appraisal of the value of the inventory and the speed at which finished goods are being sold.

(5) *Credit agencies.* These will use analyses of published accounts as one measure in their appraisment of a firm's creditworthiness.

(6) *Long-term investors, including debenture holders and existing and potential shareholders.* Whilst these parties are primarily interested in the long-term profitability of the firm, they are well aware that the deterioration of working capital can force otherwise profitable firms into liquidation. As mentioned in Chapter 1, many progressive, fast expanding firms have been bankrupted because of short-term liquidity problems. Existing shareholders may use the analyses to influence the management into adopting various policies; otherwise the analyses are used in helping decide whether the firm is worth investing in.

Solvency and Liquidity Characteristics

The major characteristics being investigated in working-capital management are solvency and liquidity. (Long-term investors may also look at working capital in order to assess its efficiency and profitability.) Profitability and gearing characteristics are not so vital in the short-term although the ability of the firm to generate annual cash flows from profits will be an important factor. The importance of liquidity in the firm to short-term creditors and bankers is that they will be relying upon payment of their debts for their own finance – the cash for these payments is only likely to come from the conversion of inventories and debtors into cash and the earning of near-term cash profits. Longer-term profitability and fixed assets will not provide immediate cash.

Analyses

The major analyses used by outside parties will be those utilising ratios and those involving forecasting future cash flows. These are dealt with below.

It is important for the firm to assess creditors' views of the company as this will help them to plan their finance-seeking strategies. For example, it is no good the firm relying upon obtaining future increases in bank overdrafts if the working-capital structure looks very dangerous (in the banker's eyes). Thus the analyses which follow should be carried out by the firm on current and forecasted data as this will help explain and anticipate creditor reaction; it may also cause management to reappraise their own strategies. Additionally, management will want to build up financial-analysis expertise themselves so that they can appraise their own debtors.

Data Sources

The main source of data available to outsiders in assessing the working-capital position of a firm is the published accounts. Although this only shows aggregated data at one day in each year, this is all that trade creditors, credit agencies and investors are likely to have access to. Only limited companies have to publish their accounts. Creditors can only request the accounts of other firms and whether this will be granted will depend partly upon the urgency of the funds required. Bankers and credit factors are often able to demand more information and may have access to the books of account; in such cases their analyses may be the same as those employed by trade creditors, only they have more detailed, more regular and more up-to-date information on which to compute them.

Apart from published accounts themselves, ratio and trend statistics are often given by trade associations and credit agencies. If the firm is being compared with many others, then use of trade statistics may be required.

In using published accounts, it must be remembered that it takes some time (often up to six months after the year end) before they become available to the public and to the analyst, employed by the bank or other creditor to assess the creditworthiness of the firm. In this period, a firm's working-capital position can alter significantly, especially if there is a dramatic economic slump, a large sudden rise in inflation or a strike. Creditors, therefore, have to use their judgement and their knowledge of prevailing conditions to account for possible changes in working-capital balances.

RATIOS

In examining published accounts for the assessment of working capital, considerable use is likely to be made of ratios as these form ready, easy-to-handle measures of performance. The main methods of using ratios are:

(1) To measure the firm's working-capital position over time. For some firms, comparisons between various subsidiaries at the same date may be tenable.

(2) To measure the firm's working capital against external yardsticks. These will usually be competing or potentially competing firms, or firms in fields which the company may enter, and relevant industrial averages.

Before commencing with a description of the major ratios, a brief mention will be given of the problems and caveats attached to ratio analysis.

Firstly, there are problems relating to the measurement of the firm's own performance over time, viz.

(1) The prior year's figures may have been exceptional because of poor or good management or because of special external events. To measure the current figures against the 'exceptional' past figures may lead to spurious interpretations unless the impact is recognised.

(2) The fact that some ratio has behaved in a particular fashion (e.g. a large increase in debtor turnover) may not by itself be indicative of good or poor performance. Consideration has to be given to what has happened to the economic factors influencing the ratio (for example, the debtor turnovers may have increased for all companies in the firm's industry and the firm may have reacted so as to be competitive). With a careful attention to the factors involved, management should be able to account for the caveats expressed in (1) and (2) above; additionally, they can compare ratios against those budgeted for. For outside analysts this will be far more difficult; they may not recognise that there were any exceptional features and even if they do they may not be able to measure the impact.

(3) Changes in accounting policies will affect the comparison of the ratios. Whilst management itself will be able to make adjustments for any changes in accounting practice, this will not be possible, or not very possible, for outsiders. The Annual Accounts should indicate the nature and extent of any changes in the profit and loss and balance-sheet figures caused by changes in accounting practice, but this will rarely be very detailed. In the majority of cases, however, and given due care, financial analysts should still be able to glean fairly reliable data from intracompany ratio analysis.

DIFFICULTIES IN MAKING INTERFIRM COMPARISONS

The problems involved with interfirm comparison are far greater than those just discussed relating to intracompany ratio analysis. Amongst the major problems are:

(1) Finding appropriate companies against which to measure performance. Even if firms are found that provide exactly similar products or services, problems may still be encountered as these firms may be of vastly different size (which can account for different ratios) or they may produce several types of goods, only one of which is produced by the firm under analysis. This caveat is also relevant when comparing firms against industry averages. These statistics, whilst of the same broad industry, will consist of a multitude of differences in relation to products, firm sizes and accounting practices.

(2) The data in published balance sheets relates to one date in the year and this, in the case of working-capital items, may not be indicative of their general nature. For example, the fireworks

manufacturer, already cited several times before, may have a very liquid balance sheet at the end of November, whilst the balance sheet of a competitor taken out at the end of September may look very weak (high inventories and high borrowings). To compare the working capital of these two companies would therefore be spurious; to attempt to adjust the figures to account for the seasonal bias would be difficult and the results tenuous.

The 'seasonality' factor is also important when looking at a company in isolation. A seemingly high 'current' ratio (described later), i.e. one which shows a lot of liquidity, could in fact be very poor for most of the year and, indeed, the firm may be very near to technical insolvency during some periods. Whilst subjective judgements can be made to account for the seasonality this will be subject to considerable uncertainty if the business is very seasonal.

Although fireworks manufacturers may be exceptional, many other businesses have some seasonal element in their activity (it is the seasonality of sales which affects working-capital balances). In the case of seasonal business, intercompany comparison should be made with firms having the same year end. Some industry statistics kept by trade associations may give regular (monthly) data on its member firms; this data is not audited, however, and this must be borne in mind when using the data.

Apart from the seasonality of data, some companies may deliberately 'window-dress' their accounts, i.e. make a special effort at one moment in the year to improve the working-capital position (it is possible to manipulate the current-asset and current-liability figures to improve the apparent position).

(3) There are various recognised methods of accounting for business transactions and these can lead to very different figures in companies' accounts. Even two companies with identical assets, sales, costs and opening working capital could end up with substantially different closing working-capital balances. One common example of differing accounting bases is the valuation of stock, e.g. L.I.F.O. (last in, first out) and F.I.F.O. (first in, first out). These can give significantly different balance-sheet valuations (and profits) in times of violent price movements (the prices of many raw material commodities are extremely erratic showing both large decreases as well as large increases in short periods of time). As firms do not state the specific valuation bases they have used, financial analysts cannot

make any adjustments. Even if the accounting bases were disclosed they could only be broad guidelines and so the analysis may still be tenuous. Another area of difficulty in analysing accounts is that some items are the result of subjective estimates. A major example in relation to working capital is the provision made for doubtful debts; this will be dependent largely on management's own attitudes *re* the conservatism of their accounts. This is another item which can create difficulties in comparing accounts; although the amounts involved may be relatively small, there is no way of assessing the impact.

Another factor that has been receiving a lot of attention of late is the impact of inflation on accounts. Although this is less marked in the case of working capital (which is usually turned over several times a year), it can still lead to some differences between reported figures and make comparisons more tenuous. The recent moves to incorporate inflation-adjusted accounts (C.C.A. accounting) into annual accounts should show the impact that inflation has on working capital; if it is significant, then adjustments to the ratios will be necessary.

TRENDS OF RATIOS

One method to help overcome some of the biases that affect intercompany comparisons is to compute the trends of ratios, these being especially relevant in the case of varying accounting bases. Unless otherwise stated the accounting policies adopted by limited companies should be consistent over time, thus comparing trends of ratios should show the relative performance; trends may also help reduce the uncertainty surrounding the ratios of seasonal businesses. Analysts could also attempt to extrapolate trends of ratios by using some time-series forecasting method. There have been no reports of this type of analysis having been undertaken but it does represent a potential development.

The analyst should be aware of the above caveats in the interpretations of ratios but, by using experience and judgement, he should be able to place a fair amount of reliance on them. The major liquidity ratios are outlined below.

Current ratio

This is the ratio of current assets to current liabilities and is expressed thus:

$$\frac{\text{current assets}}{\text{current liabilities}}$$

From the balance sheet shown in Table 6.1 the current ratio is 1·875. The ratio is used as a major indicator of the firm's ability to meet its debts, this being the main concern of short-term lenders to the company. Thus, can creditors and bank overdrafts be repaid from cash, the realisation of debts and the sale of inventory? The traditional norm for the current ratio has been 2, although individual

Table 6.1 *Balance Sheet as at 31 December 1975*

	£	£	£
Issued share capital			100,000
Profit and loss account			210,000
			310,000
10% loan stock			50,000
			360,000
Represented by:			
Fixed assets			220,000
Current assets			
Inventories		110,000	
Accounts receivables		130,000	
Marketable securities		20,000	
Cash		40,000	
		300,000	
Less current liabilities			
Trade creditors	70,000		
Taxation	50,000		
Bank overdraft	40,000		
		160,000	140,000
			£360,000

companies may have ratios anywhere in the range 1·5–2·5; if a firm has operated very satisfactorily for a number of years on a current ratio of 1·5, then this implies that 1·5 is a satisfactory ratio for the particular company. The higher the ratio the more liquid the company is; at the same time, however, it often indicates lower profitability (e.g. less free credit being taken from trade suppliers than is possible).

The analyst should be aware of practices that can lead to a substantial improvement in the current ratio. For example, if current assets were realised and £150,000 of the current liabilities were repaid, the current ratio would rise to 15 (current assets = £150,000, current liabilities = £10,000). The analyst should therefore look at the absolute figures when considering the interpretation of ratios; any practices such as that above should then be obvious. This practice can also distort other ratios but its main impact is likely to be upon the current ratio.

Quick-assets ratio

Another liquidity ratio which is in very common use is the quick assets or acid test. This is computed thus:

$$\frac{\text{current assets} - \text{inventories}}{\text{current liabilities}}$$

and the quick-assets test ratio for the balance sheet in Table 6.1 is 1·1875. The reason for omitting inventories from the numerator is that these usually take some time to realise and they will not therefore be available to meet immediate or near-future debts. Many companies have several months' stock on hand and even sales at reduced prices may take some time to achieve. Whilst debtors often amount to, say, two months of credit sales, it is usually possible to factor them or borrow against them (the pledging of inventory, however, cannot be taken for granted).

The quick-assets ratio is, therefore, a much more sensitive guide to immediate technical solvency. If possible, derivations to the above ratios could be made, e.g. including some part of inventory (i.e. that expected to be sold in the next two weeks) and ignoring some current liabilities (i.e. taxation due in, say, six months' time). These may be difficult to compute from the data given in published accounts but, if the analyst is confident in his information, then he could use adaptations and improve the sensitivity of the results. Another factor that should be incorporated into the current and quick-assets ratios is the overdraft facilities that are available to the firm but which have not yet been used up. The availability of these facilities provides further sources of finance for paying the firm's suppliers but, unfortunately, it is very exceptional for a company to disclose its overdraft standby facilities. There are also sound arguments for including any marketable investments held for the long-term (and therefore disclosed separately from the current-assets grouping) in the current ratio; whilst held primarily for the long-term, these investments can still be realised immediately to provide cash with which to repay creditors and bankers.

Daily cash flows

Another useful liquidity statistic is to calculate the daily cash inflow of the firm from its normal trading operations. For example, a firm may have annual profits after tax of £400,000 and depreciation of £100,000. One measure of daily cash flow is:

$$\frac{\text{net profits} + \text{depreciation}}{\text{number of trading days per year (say 250)}}$$

(Depreciation does not involve any cash outflow.)

For the example the ratio is:

$$\frac{400{,}000 + 100{,}000}{250}$$
$$= £2000 \text{ a day}$$

Although this is a somewhat crude method, the reader will easily recognise the assumptions involved in this statistic which does give some indication of the daily cash-flow generation. If, for example, the current liabilities exceeded current assets (a serious position) the daily cash-flow generation would indicate how many trading days it would take to remedy the situation (conversion to calendar days could easily be made if necessary), e.g. if current liabilities were £200,000 and current assets were £170,000, it would take 15 trading days (i.e. (200,000–170,000)/2000 = 15) before the deficit would be cleared. If the company was in a loss-making position the daily negative cash flows would show, for example, how long it would be before the current ratio dipped below 1; if the current assets are £400,000, current liabilities are £340,000 and the daily negative cash flow is £3000, then in 20 days the current ratio will reduce to below 1. Various derivatives of the above can also be used; for example, the number of daily net cash inflows from normal operations that are needed to repay trade creditors or, perhaps, total current liabilities can be computed. Thus, if the firm's cash was exhausted and if inventories and debtors were unrealisable, then the creditors will know how long it will take for them to be repaid from the company's normal operations.

Empirical research into the prediction of bankruptcies by ratio analysis

Some empirical research has been conducted into the prediction of bankruptcies of firms by using ratio analysis. The major study is that by Altman[1] in the United States who extracted 22 ratios from two groups of firms, one group which became insolvent and the other group which did not. He used discriminant analysis techniques (discussed briefly in Chapter 3 when used to predict 'good' customers to whom credit should be given) to ascertain the ratios which efficiently predicted bankruptcies. This resulted in five ratios which significantly discriminated between bankruptcies and non-bankruptcies. Thus, if the ratios for the five variables moved beyond certain levels, this indicated a high probability of an ensuing bankruptcy. These were:

(1) $\dfrac{\text{retained earnings}}{\text{total assets}}$;

(2) $\dfrac{\text{earnings before interest and taxes}}{\text{total assets}}$;

(3) $\dfrac{\text{market value of equity shares}}{\text{book value of total debt}}$;

(4) $\dfrac{\text{sales}}{\text{total assets}}$;

(5)

$$\frac{\text{working capital (defined as current assets} - \text{current liabilities)}}{\text{total assets}}$$

The last ratio, the liquidity variable, was found to be more useful for prediction purposes than either the quick-assets test or the current ratio. Altman's discriminant model provided very accurate results with 94 per cent of bankruptcies being predicted, and correct overall groupings (that is both bankruptcies and non-bankruptcies) being predicted in 95 per cent of cases. The author claimed that the ratios used in the model were able to predict many business failures up to two years before they occurred.

Altman's model emphasised that in considering the solvency of a company a number of factors (ratios) have to be considered and that profitability, not liquidity, was perhaps the major item. (The major ratio contributing to the discrimination of bankrupt–non-bankrupt groupings was found to be: (earnings before interest and taxes/total assets).) Thus a firm with profitable current operations is likely to be able to avoid bankruptcy even if its liquidity position, as evidenced by its current ratio, is poor. So apart from the ratios discussed in this chapter, others also need to be considered in assessing a firm's ability to pay its debts.

Other ratios

The other working-capital ratios mentioned in the text will also be used in helping determine the firm's solvency. The major ratios covered have been inventory turnover (Chapter 2) and debtor turnover (Chapter 3). In certain cases, a creditor may be able to demand greater information than that given in the annual accounts. For example, a credit factor may obtain data relating to the age profile of debts and the bad debts to sale ratios; in addition, various efficiency and profitability ratios will be found useful, see (Westwick[2]).

SOURCES AND USES OF FUNDS STATEMENT

Another analysis that can be used to help evaluate a firm's cash-flow position is to compute, from the published accounts, a sources and uses of funds statement (sometimes called sources and application of funds statement, the financing table, cash-flow statement, or funds statement). This shows funds generated during the period from all sources (e.g. profits before depreciation, capital issues, increases in current liabilities, decreases in current assets, proceeds from the sale of capital assets) and the total uses of funds (increases in fixed assets and current assets, repayments of loan capital, dividends). The balance between the sources and uses represents the movement in the cash balance.

An example of a sources and uses of funds statement is shown in Table 6.2. This shows that cash has increased by £130,000 which appears satisfactory; however, when examining the statement the analyst can see that this increase was more than accounted for by the issue of new shares and loan capital during the year. It is unlikely that this source of finance will be available next year and so, other things remaining the same, there will be a large cash deficit. Of course, the fixed-asset expansion which took place in the year to 31 December 1975 may be cut back and so a liquidity crisis averted.

The sources and uses of funds statement is a useful analysis for short-term lenders to make as it identifies the make-up of the cash balances. This is not readily apparent from the published profit and loss accounts and balance sheets. When the statement is allied to the analyst's opinions of the firm's prospects and the computed ratios, a future cash-flow profile can be forecast. On the basis of these analyses and forecasts, creditors and bankers should be able to make a reasonable appraisement of a firm's creditworthiness.

Table 6.2 *Sources and uses of Funds Statement for the year ended 31 December 1975*

Sources		£	£
Profit after taxation		150,000	
Depreciation		30,000	180,000
Proceeds from the issue of 100,000 ordinary shares at £2 each		200,000	
Proceeds from the issue of debenture stock		100,000	
			300,000
Proceeds from the sale of a subsidiary company			20,000
Increase in current liabilities:			
Creditors		10,000	
Taxation		20,000	
			30,000
			530,000
Uses			
Purchase of fixed assets		230,000	
Repayment of loan		30,000	
Increase in current assets:			
Inventory	£80,000		
Debtors	60,000		
		140,000	400,000
INCREASE IN CASH BALANCES			£130,000

Many companies are now incorporating sources and uses of funds statements in their annual accounts and so the analysis is readily available to credit assessors. This has partly been occasioned by the Accounting Standards Steering Committee (comprising the senior accounting bodies in the U.K.) who have recently issued an exposure draft[3] recommending the use of the statement by companies and suggesting a form of presentation.

Summary

The analyses and methodologies presented in this chapter should enable management to assess corporate customers' working-capital positions from published data. Once having established basic ratios and liquidity statistics, management can then subjectively determine the riskiness of their potential customers and give credit or otherwise accordingly. As stated earlier in the chapter, it will also be useful for the firm to assess its own working-capital position from published data as this may help them anticipate their own creditors' and potential creditors' actions.

CHAPTER 7

Short-Term Forecasting Methods

Forecasting is a vital ingredient in the making of both long-term and short-term plans. For example, in the control and management of working capital we are attempting to optimise the future profitability–risk profile of the firm and this will require, amongst other things, forecasts of the future demand for inventory, the level of future interest rates and the availability of future finance. Many of the formal decision models discussed previously in the book rely on forecasts of demand functions as one input and the 'optimal' solutions produced therefrom are dependent upon the forecasting accuracy. The focal point for the planning of working capital is the sales forecast; from this, fairly reliable assumptions can be made as regards the management of inventory, debtors, cash and their funding. Table 7.1 shows the relationships between the sales figures

Table 7.1 *Relationships of working-capital items to sales*

Inventories of raw materials, work in progress and finished goods	= f (production) = f(sales).
Accounts receivables	= f(sales, credit terms given).
Cash balances	= f(realisation of accounts receivables, payments for trading and operating expenses).
	= f(sales, credit terms given, credit terms received).
Finance raised	= f(cash shortages (which is a function of above), banking conditions, firm's creditworthiness).

f = function of.

and the various components of working capital – clearly sales has an extremely important impact.

In the past, sales forecasts have often amounted to simple intuitive guesses without any analysis of underlying patterns of influencing variables; for example, a typical sales forecast made by a small to medium-sized firm may have been 'last year's sales plus 5 per cent'. However, there now exist a wide range of quantitative forecasting techniques which can be readily and easily applied to sales. These improved techniques have led to increased accuracy, explicit statements of the uncertainty surrounding the forecast, specified probabilistic outcomes, and tested for sensitivity. Many are simple to apply and there is little excuse nowadays for management not adopting these methods.

For working-capital purposes it is essentially short-term forecasts that are required; if possible, these should be period-by-period, especially if sales are seasonal. There are two main categories of quantitative forecasting techniques which are relevant for short-term sales estimates: time-series analysis and regression (the third, qualitative forecasting, is essentially long-term). In addition, various other guidelines are available such as orders on hand (often found in engineering industries or capital goods manufacturers) and salesmen's forecasts; these will be dealt with later.

Time Series

Time-series models consist of establishing patterns in an historical series of data and extrapolating these trends and patterns into the future. The models are based on the assumption that the pattern will recur over time; this has more validity in the short-term and thus time-series analysis is appropriate for short-term forecasting situations.

Time-series models are constructed by taking sequential historical recordings of the factor being forecast and establishing a pattern or relationship over time. Having established a pattern, this is then projected into the future in accordance with the relationship. The data required for time-series models of sales is often readily available in most companies as accountants traditionally record information in a sequential manner. For a firm which produces a number of different products, a separate model for each will be required.

The major time-series methods are outlined below. For a detailed review of these specialised texts should be consulted.[1,2,7]

TREND FITTING

This is where the data is tested to see if it fits a specific type of curve or trend relationship; if it does, then the curve or trend is extrapolated to give the forecast. Examples of curve relationships include the following:

Curve	*Equation*	*Description*
Exponential	$Y = ab^T$	This causes Y to increase by a constant rate – it is thus the equation for geometric progression
Simple polynomial	$Y = a + bT$	A straight line
Second degree polynomial	$Y = a + bT + cT^2$	A parabola
Higher degree polynomials	$Y = a + bT + cT^2 + dT^3 \ldots$	
Simple modified exponential	$Y = a + bc^T$	The exponential trend growth rate at some stage declines and becomes asymptotic to a certain value
Gompertz	$Y = ab^{CT}$, or in logarithmic form: $\log Y = \log a + (\log b)c^T$	The percentage rate of growth changes by a constant proportion from period to period until an asymptote is. reached
Logistic	$\frac{1}{Y} = a + bc$	A modified exponential curve where the formula calculates the reciprocal of Y

NOTE: Many of the above can be computed in log-form.

The application of trend fitting involves arranging data in a time sequential order. Various trend equations are then applied to the data to see if they are relevant. The methods can be applied for both short and medium-term forecasts; long-term forecasts (say five to ten years) can be made although they are likely to suffer a highish degree of inaccuracy.

MOVING AVERAGE

This is a method whereby an average of past recordings is plotted. This smooths a time series and can be useful in highlighting the underlying trend of an erratic variable.

EXPONENTIAL SMOOTHING

This is a moving average where the items are given descending weights the further they are from today. The model can be expressed as

$$S_t(x) = ax_t + (1 - a)S_{t-1}(x),$$

where x_t = the value of the series in time period t,
$S_t(x)$ = smoothed value (moving average) of the series in time period t,
$S_{t-1}(x)$ = smoothed value (moving average) of the series in time immediately prior to period t,
a = smoothing constant, $0 < a < 1$.

Thus the new forecast is a function (a) of the latest recording and a function ($1 - a$) of the last forecast. Exponential smoothing represents a significant advance on the simple moving-average formula as it gives greater weight to more recent data.

CLASSIFICATION OF TIME-SERIES MOVEMENTS

Time-series movements of many economic data have certain common characteristics. These are longer-term trends, cyclical movements within the long-term trend (possibly the trade cycle), seasonal movements within the cycle (possibly the periods of the year) and random or irregular movements. Thus a time series (Y) can be represented in the following way.

$$Y = T \times C \times S + R,$$

where T = trend,
C = cyclical,
S = seasonal,
R = random.

(This is the common multiplicative model. Some statisticians may prefer the additive model (where T, C, S and R are added) in certain situations.)

A common analysis of the time series involves decomposing it into its component items. There are numerous methods for decomposition, these mainly using some form of moving-average or percentage method (the analysis for trend would probably incorporate regression analysis).

There also exist a number of more sophisticated forecasting techniques and the interested reader should consult Firth (reference made earlier) for a brief description of these. One which is rapidly gaining acceptance and deserves further mention is the Box–Jenkins method (reference made above). This is particularly suited to forecasting situations where the basic underlying pattern is not apparent. The method involves checking whether various 'tentative' models (or patterns) are applicable to the data; when a model is found that approximates to the data, then this is used to generate forecasts.

Causal Models (Econometric Models – Regression Analysis)

Causal models are equations which express the relationship of the item being forecast (the dependent variable) with a number of independent variables which have some determining influence on the dependent variable; the model thus expresses mathematically the inherent causal relationships. For example, a causal model for sales of a domestic appliance may include as independent variables, relative prices to those of competitors, real growth in consumers' income, the number of retail outlets, relative advertising expenditure and hire-purchase facilities. The model can be described notationally as:

$$\text{sales} = aRP + bCI + cRO + dAD + eHP$$

where RP = relative price,
CI = real growth in consumers' income,
RO = number of retail outlets,
AD = relative advertising expenditure,
HP = hire-purchase terms,
a, b, c, d, e = the weights attached to the above factors (known as regression coefficients).

By using past data the above relationships can be quantified and the significance of the complete model as a prediction device can be ascertained. The model is derived by determining and testing the likely causal relationships until a statistically satisfactory 'fit' has been found. Many of the firm's executives are likely to be involved in helping derive the model although the statistical testing will be left to the expert personnel. It should be recognised that it is likely to be revised across time as experience is gained and as relationships change.

The forecasting is done by either using forecasts of the independent variables or by using historical measures of the independent variables where the item being forecast is in a lagged relationship thereto. These values on the right-hand side of the equation then give a value for the dependent variable being forecast. If the independent variables have themselves to be forecast, then the model presumes these are easier to do than the dependent variable itself; if not, or if the independent variables are difficult to estimate anyway, then the model is almost certainly going to be of little use in forecasting. Lagged relationships might include, say, the demand for replacement car tyres being partially dependent upon new car registrations made within the last year, the last two, three and four years (by determining the replacement age range of tyres and the number of tyres in use, a forecast of the future demand can be made). Similarly, bathroom-equipment manufacturers may base their near-future sales forecasts partially on the knowledge of the number of new housing units started in the prior year.

Causal models allow various statistical measures to be calculated, e.g. confidence limits expressing the likely variability of the outcomes and tests of significance can be automatically calculated for the model. This type of data gives much more information to the manager and, in addition, the model can be interrogated to test for the sensitivity of the results to different business and economic assumptions. Causal models are excellent techniques for short and medium-term forecasting (contrasting with time-series methods which are generally only valid in the short-term), for the ascertaining of major turning points and for giving forecasts of the likely impact of a major policy or operational decision that is being contemplated by management. This latter point represents an important advantage of causal models over time-series methods. Although a time-series relationship may fit very precisely over some historical time period, the introduction of, say, a quantity and cash discount for the first time may render the relationship quite useless. A regression model, however, allows such variables to be incorporated (although it may be no easy task to establish valid weights for the factors). One factor that is often incorporated is a relative price variable; for goods that have high elasticities of demand any movement in its pricing, relative to other goods, will have a significant impact on quantity sales.

Causal models are the most costly to construct and operate and they often require considerable human effort in data collection. An additional constraint on these models is that they are fairly sophisticated and managers may need some training in interpreting the results.

Applications of Regression Forecasting

Causal models have been adopted by the Electricity Council in forecasting industrial and domestic electricity consumption.[3] The models used were thus:

$$\log E_t^i = 0{\cdot}261 \log Y_t + 0{\cdot}866 \log E^i{}_{t-1} + \text{seasonal constants}$$
$$\log E_t^d = 1{\cdot}616 \log C_t - 0{\cdot}408 \log P_t - 0{\cdot}008\ T_t + 0{\cdot}553 \log E_{t-1}^d + \text{seasonal constants},$$

in which E_t^i = industrial electricity consumption in time period t,
Y_t = index of industrial production in time period t,
E_t^d = domestic electricity consumption in time period t,
C_t = consumers' expenditure at constant prices,
P_t = price index of electricity rates relative to index of other fuel prices,
T_t = deviation about mean temperature, degrees Fahrenheit.

The underlying rationale to the equations is that electricity consumption is influenced not only by current factors, such as industrial production and consumer expenditure, but also by past values of these factors. This explains why each equation contains the dependent variable, in lagged form (i.e. for the prior period), on the right-hand side as an explanatory variable. Both equations fitted the data extremely well, the coefficients of determination being 0·996 and 0·987 respectively for the quarterly data from 1955 to 1965. The forecaster then needed to make forecasts for the explanatory variables Y_t, C_t, P_t and T_t. This was no easy task but they were considered more predictable than electricity consumption itself.

Another example relates to the British car industry. In 1961, the National Institute of Economic and Social Research[4] used the following equation to forecast home car demand in 1965:

$$\Delta \log S_t = 1{\cdot}503\,\Delta \log Y_t - 0{\cdot}0012\,\Delta \log P_t - 0{\cdot}0238\,\Delta \log H_t + 0{\cdot}0085 + 0{\cdot}3638\,\Delta \log S_{t-1},$$

where S_t = actual stock level per head at time t,
Y_t = real personal disposable income per head at time t,
P_t = index of car prices (second-hand) divided by the overall consumer price index,
H_t = hire-purchase variable,
Δ = change from year to year.

The equation incorporated the major items one would expect to influence car demand. The coefficient of determination over the period 1947–60 was 0·768 and this represents a fairly good 'fit'; however, testing the model also found that neither the hire-purchase variable nor the price variable contributed significantly.

Some other interesting studies of the applications of causal model building in forecasting sales are contained in the works by Harberger[5] and Cowling.[6] One study quoted in Harberger is that conducted by Burstein relating to the demand for household refrigerators. The independent variables in this study were a replacement factor (he took the stock of refrigerators and applied a rate of depreciation to this) and consumers' real income. A similar study quoted in Harberger was that by Chow, who sought to forecast automobile demand by regressing it with a 'stock' of existing cars and disposable and expected income.

Simulation

Many processes involve a number of variables, each of which has a probability distribution. These are often too complicated to be represented in equation form and use has to be made of simulation techniques, which require a considerable amount of historical data (or forecasts) relating to the possible outcomes and their probability of occurrence; also required is a model of the process showing the relationships between the variables. Once this has been achieved for the various variables in the process, the simulation (known as Monte Carlo simulation) is conducted by using random numbers to generate possible probabilities of total outcomes. Using a computer the model is run several thousand times, after which a probabilistic distribution of outcomes is achieved. Various statistical distributions can be input into the model which specify the interaction between variables in a process.

Simulation exercises have been used fairly often in determining optimum inventory policies and controls, especially, for example, where probabilistic data exists in relation to demand and lead time. Simulation has also been used effectively in the management of accounts receivable and cash.

Selecting a Technique

The various techniques discussed in this chapter are all applicable to short-term sales forecasting. The major advantage of time-series models is that they are relatively cheap and are fairly easy to construct. Causal models, however, can give longer-term forecasts, express the variability of outcomes and can incorporate the impact of new policy decisions, but the time and work involved in building these models can be quite extensive and thus it is only larger firms who have adopted these techniques to date.

The selection of an appropriate technique depends partly upon its cost and the data requirements; the other main criterion is the forecasting ability of the technique. In order to find, say, an appropriate time-series technique the various methods will have to be applied on the firm's historical data in order to test the goodness of fit and to assess past forecasting accuracy. Many companies will employ a statistics or operational research department and these will contain personnel skilled in the practice of forecasting. In the absence of specialised departments, however, there is no reason why the existing staff should not be able to utilise the basic methods, especially as there are many computer packages relating to their use.

Salesmen's Judgement and Forward Order Positions

Combined with the forecasts produced by the quantitative techniques described above should be the salesmen's subjective judgement of demand. Salesmen's judgement is likely to be fairly reliable in the very short term and should therefore be utilised in forecasting and planning. Another item which has to be incorporated along with the forecast is the forward order position. In certain industries it is common for most sales to be the result of prior-placed orders (i.e. one-off engineering jobs). In other industries or trades (e.g. consumer durables) a fair amount of sales may be represented by forward orders; these forward-order statistics should be incorporated into the short-term forecasting process.

Utilising the Sales Forecast in Cash Budgeting

Once the short-term sales forecast has been made, the accountant should then be able to construct a cash budget as in Chapter 4. The expected cash receipts are determined by applying the credit terms granted by the firm to the forecast sales; past experience as regards the taking of discounts and of customers taking beyond the period of credit to pay, will also need to be incorporated.

The production department will draw up schedules relating to the sales forecasts, showing raw-material requirements, labour requirements and other variable expenses. (These schedules will incorporate any build-up or run-down of inventory levels.) The accountant will know of the fixed expenses incurred in running the factory and will likewise be able to compute the fixed and variable administrative and selling expenses. The cash-payments schedule can then be prepared using the expenses forecasts and the credit terms taken by the firm.

The difference between the cash receipts and cash payments for each period (possibly weekly or monthly) is then computed over some planning-time horizon. Non-regular expenditures such as taxes, dividends and capital expenditures, and non-regular receipts such as proceeds from an issue of shares, can then be included in the cash budget (these items will be known several months in advance).

On analysis of the expected cash flows, management may decide to adopt new policies as regards the expansion–contraction of sales, inventories and accounts receivable. This in turn may mean revised sales forecasts, adjusting for the new policies, and revised cash budgets. Clearly, however, these revisions and plans are all based on the firm's sales estimates – its correct forecasting is therefore of major importance in the management and control of working capital. Forecasting methods can also be applied to all the various factors of a company's operations instead of applying fixed relationships to the level of sales (e.g. labour supply and cost, raw-material prices, interest rates). This, however, involves a lot of work and will require sophisticated corporate models to be built; the forecasting techniques will be those discussed above.

References

Chapter 2

1. J. McN. Stancill, *The Management of Working Capital* (International Textbook Company, 1971).

2. C. D. Lewis, *Scientific Inventory Control* (Butterworth, 1970).

3. K. G. Lockyer, *Stock Control: A Practical Approach* (Cassell, 1972).

4. M. K. Starr and D. W. Miller, *Inventory Control: Theory and Practice* (Prentice-Hall, 1962).

5. E. G. Brisch and Partners, *Classification and Coding in the Service of Industry* (BIM, 1966).

6. E. A. Haworth, 'Group Technology – Using the Opitz System', *Production Engineering*, 47, 1 (January 1968).

7. A. Snyder, 'Principles of Inventory Management', *Financial Executive* (April 1964).

8. R. G. Brown, *Decision Rules for Inventory Management* (Holt, Rinehart & Winston, 1967).

9. R. Bellman, *Dynamic Programming* (Princeton University Press, 1967).

10. E. Naddor, *Inventory Systems* (Wiley, 1966).

Chapter 3

1. J. H. Myers and E. W. Forgy, 'The Development of Numerical Credit Evaluation Systems', *Journal of the American Statistical Association*, 58 (September 1963).

2. W. Beranek, *Analysis for Financial Decisions* (Irwin, 1963).

3. M. Mitchner and P. R. Peterson, 'An Operations Research Study of the Collection of Defaulted Loans', *Operations Research*, 5 (August 1957).

4. R. M. Cyert, H. J. Davidson and G. L. Thompson, 'Estimation

of the Allowance for Doubtful Accounts by Markov Chains', *Management Science*, 8 (April 1962).

Chapter 4

1. J. M. Keynes, *The General Theory of Employment, Interest and Money* (Harcourt, 1935).
2. W. J. Baumol, 'The Transactions Demand for Cash: An Inventory Theoretic Approach', *Quarterly Journal of Economics* (November 1952).
3. M. H. Miller and D. Orr, 'A Model of the Demand for Money by Firms', *Quarterly Journal of Economics* (August 1966).
4. M. H. Miller and D. Orr, 'An Application of Control Limit Models to the Management of Corporate Cash Balances', *Proceedings of the Conference on Financial Research and its Implications for Management*, ed. A. A. Robichek (Wiley, 1967).
5. W. Beranek, *Analysis for Financial Decisions* (Irwin, 1963).
6. D. J. White and J. M. Norman, 'Control of Cash Reserves', *Operational Research Quarterly*, 16, 3 (September 1965).
7. J. McN. Stancill, 'The Determination of Corporate Holdings of Cash and Marketable Securities' in *Financial Decision Making*, ed. E. J. Mock (International Textbook Company, 1967).
8. E. J. Mock and D. Shuckett, 'Increasing the Velocity of Corporate Funds', *Management Services* (July–August 1966).
9. J. McN. Stancill, 'A Lock-Box Model', *Management Science*, 15, 2 (October 1968).
10. R. L. Ackoff and M. W. Sasieni, *Fundamentals of Operational Research* (Wiley, 1968).
11. G. Cooper and R. J. Cridlan, *Law and Procedure of the Stock Exchange* (Butterworth, 1971).
12. M. A. Firth, *Investment Analysis* (Harper & Row, 1975).
13. T. Ryan, *Portfolio Analysis* (Macmillan, forthcoming).

Chapter 5

1. K. Midgley and R. G. Burns, *Institutions of the Capital Market* (Macmillan, forthcoming).
2. P. Einzig, *The Euro-dollar System* (Macmillan, 1970).
3. W. G. Lewellen, *The Cost of Capital* (Wadsworth Publishing Company, 1969).

4. A. A. Robichek, D. Teichroew and J. M. Jones, 'Optimal Short-Term Financing Decisions', *Management Science*, 12 (September 1965). *See also* A. A. Robichek and S. C. Myers, *Optimal Financing Decisions* (Prentice-Hall, 1965).

Chapter 6

1. E. I. Altman, 'Financial ratios, discriminant analysis and the prediction of corporate bankruptcy', *Journal of Finance* (September 1968).

2. C. A. Westwick, *How to Use Management Ratios* (Gower Press, 1973).

3. *Statement of source and application of funds*, A.S.S.C. Exposure draft, ED13 (April 1974).

Chapter 7

1. G. E. P. Box and G. M. Jenkins, *Time Series Forecasting and Control* (Holden Day, 1968).

2. I.C.I., *Mathematical Trend Curves: An Aid to Forecasting*, I.C.I. Monograph, No. 1 (Oliver & Boyd, 1964).

3. The Electricity Council, *Economic Planning and Electricity Forecasting* (1966).

4. 'Prospects for the British Car Industry', *National Institute Economic Review*, 17 (September 1971). *See also* 'Long Term Forecasts of Demand for Cars, Selected Consumer Durables, and Energy', *National Institute Economic Review*, 40 (May 1967).

5. A. Harberger, *The Demand for Durable Goods* (University of Chicago Press, 1960).

6. K. Cowling, *Market Structure and Corporate Behaviour* (Gray-Mills Publishing Ltd, 1972).

7. M. A. Firth, *Forecasting Methods for Management* (Edward Arnold, 1976).

Index

2292907